Health Professionals and Trust

T0200527

An ever increasing number of codes of conduct, disciplinary bodies, ethics committees and bureaucratic policies now prescribe how health professionals and health researchers relate to their patients. In this book, Mark Henaghan argues that the result of this trend towards heightened regulation has been to undermine the traditional dynamic of trust in health professionals and to diminish reliance upon their professional judgment, whilst simultaneously failing to trust patients to make decisions about their own care.

This book examines the issue of health professionals and trust comparatively in a number of countries including the USA, Canada, Australia, New Zealand and the UK. The book draws upon historical analysis of legislation, case law, disciplinary proceedings reports, articles in medical and law journals and protocols produced by management teams in hospitals, to illustrate the ways in which there has been a discernible shift away from trust in healthcare professionals. Henaghan argues that this erosion of trust has the potential to dehumanise the unique relationship that has traditionally existed between healthcare professionals and their patients, thereby running the risk of turning healthcare into a mechanistic enterprise controlled by 'management processes' rather than a humanistic relationship governed by trust and judgment.

This book is an invaluable resource for students and scholars of medical law and medical sociology, public policy-makers and a range of associated professionals, from health-service managers to medical science and clinical researchers.

Mark Henaghan is Dean and Professor of Law at the University of Otago, Dunedin, New Zealand. He specialises in Family Law and is a Barrister and Solicitor of the High Court of New Zealand.

Biomedical Law and Ethics Library
Series Editor: Sheila A.M. McLean

Scientific and clinical advances, social and political developments and the impact of healthcare on our lives raise profound ethical and legal questions. Medical law and ethics have become central to our understanding of these problems, and are important tools for the analysis and resolution of problems – real or imagined.

In this series, scholars at the forefront of biomedical law and ethics contribute to the debates in this area, with accessible, thought-provoking and sometimes controversial ideas. Each book in the series develops an independent hypothesis and argues cogently for a particular position. One of the major contributions of this series is the extent to which both law and ethics are utilised in the content of the books and the shape of the series itself.

The books in this series are analytical, with a key target audience of lawyers, doctors, nurses and the intelligent lay public.

Available titles:

Human Fertilisation and Embryology (2006)
Reproducing Regulation
Kirsty Horsey & Hazel Biggs

Intention and Causation in Medical Non-Killing (2006)
The Impact of Criminal Law Concepts on Euthanasia and Assisted Suicide
Glenys Williams

Impairment and Disability (2007)
Law and Ethics at the Beginning and End of Life
Sheila McLean & Laura Williamson

Bioethics and the Humanities (2007)
Attitudes and Perceptions
Robin Downie & Jane Macnaughton

Defending the Genetic Supermarket (2007)
The Law and Ethics of Selecting the Next Generation
Colin Gavaghan

The Harm Paradox (2007)
Tort Law and the Unwanted Child in an Era of Choice
Nicolette Priaulx

Assisted Dying (2007)
Reflections on the Need for Law Reform
Sheila McLean

Medicine, Malpractice and Misapprehensions (2007)
Vivienne Harpwood

Euthanasia, Ethics and the Law (2007)
From Conflict to Compromise
Richard Huxtable

Best Interests of the Child in Healthcare (2007)
Sarah Elliston

Values in Medicine (2008)
The Realities of Clinical Practice
Donald Evans

Autonomy, Consent and the Law (2009)
Sheila McLean

Healthcare Research Ethics and Law (2009)
Regulation, Review and Responsibility
Hazel Biggs

The Body in Bioethics (2009)
Alastair V. Campbell

Genomic Negligence (2011)
An Interest in Autonomy as the Basis for Novel Negligence Claims
Generated by Genetic Technology
Victoria Chico

Health Professionals and Trust
The Cure for Healthcare Law and Policy
Mark Henaghan

Forthcoming titles include:

Abortion Law and Policy
An Equal Opportunity Perspective
Kerry Petersen

Bioethics
Methods, Theories, Scopes
Marcus Düwell

Birth, Harm and the Role of Distributive Justice
Burdens, Blessings, Need and Desert
Alasdair Maclean

Medicine and Law at the Limits of Life
Clinical Ethics in Action
Richard Huxtable

The Jurisprudence of Pregnancy
Concepts of Conflict, Persons and Property
Mary Ford

About the Series Editor

Professor Sheila McLean is International Bar Association Professor of Law and Ethics in Medicine and Director of the Institute of Law and Ethics in Medicine at the University of Glasgow.

Health Professionals and Trust

The Cure for Healthcare
Law and Policy

Mark Henaghan

 Routledge
Taylor & Francis Group

LONDON AND NEW YORK

First published 2012
by Routledge
2 Park Square, Milton Park, Abingdon, Oxon OX14 4RN

Simultaneously published in the USA and Canada
by Routledge
711 Third Avenue, New York, NY 10017

Routledge is an imprint of the Taylor & Francis Group, an informa business

British Library Cataloguing in Publication Data
A catalogue record for this book is available from the British Library

Library of Congress Cataloging in Publication Data
    Henaghan, Mark.
    Health professionals and trust: the cure for healthcare law and
    policy/Mark Henaghan.
        p. cm. – (Biomedical law & ethics library)
    Includes bibliographical references and index.
    ISBN 978-0-415-49581-3 (hardback) – ISBN 978-0-415-49582-0
    (paperback) 1. Medical care – Law and legislation. 2. Medical
    personnel and patient. 3. Communication in medicine. 4. Medical
    personnel – Discipline. 5. Patients – Legal status, laws, etc.
    6. Medical ethics. I. Title.
    K3601.H46 2011
    344.03'21—dc22

                                                        2011015876

ISBN: 978–0–415–49581–3 (hbk)
ISBN: 978–0–415–49582–0 (pbk)
ISBN: 978–0–203–69709–2 (ebk)

Typeset in Garamond
by RefineCatch Limited, Bungay, Suffolk

Contents

Acknowledgements

Thank you for her love and support to my wife, Aimy, who trusted me to finish.

Thank you to Alice Irving, Daniel Eyre and Ruth Ballantyne for their invaluable research assistance. James Ellison and Ruth Ballantyne turned illegible handwriting into script, provided editorial suggestions and kept me on track. Ruth Ballantyne checked all of the footnotes and references before final submission, a painstaking task I am most grateful for. Thank you to Michael Holland for his impeccable proofreading. Thank you to Karen Warrington, my executive assistant, who kept all my work up to date so I had the time to complete this book. My colleagues in the Otago Law Faculty who, through their conversations, repartee and passing on helpful material, greatly enriched my understanding of trust. Thank you. The editorial team at Routledge were incredibly patient and highly professional. Thank you to the peer reviewers who believed that this was a worthwhile project.

Preface

What would healthcare law and policy look like if it were driven by the central idea of establishing trust between healthcare professionals and their patients? This book attempts to answer this question. It does so by first establishing why trust is important in healthcare relationships, and why it is currently under threat. It then turns to the philosophers to define what trust is and how it can best be assured. The emergency situation, complaints procedure, relationships between health professionals and between health professionals and their patients and the families of sick children are analysed using trust as the guiding principle.

The discovery of the human genome has led to new ways of working in medical research whereby gene mutations and markers are indicators of future health. Francis Collins, one of the discoverers of the human genome, has called the sequence of genes that make up our human genome 'the language of God' because of the beautiful symmetry of it all.[1] The perception that we may be 'playing God' by delving into the essence of our DNA has created the potential for distrust between healthcare researchers and their communities. Trust has been abused in this quest for new knowledge, particularly with regard to indigenous communities around the world. Yet trust is essential if we are going to use this new knowledge for the good of everyone.

In order for healthcare systems to be trusted and more effective, the final chapter shows they must be more equitable and accessible to all members of the particular society, not just those who can afford them.

Two remarkable female philosophers have been the inspiration and guiding light for this book. Annette Baier, a graduate of my own university, the University of Otago in Dunedin, New Zealand, who taught moral philosophy for years at the University of Pittsburgh in the United States, has thought deeply about what trust is and how we might know who we can trust. Annette says those who attempt to equalise power with us are likely to be the most trustworthy.

Onora O'Neill, Professor of Moral Philosophy at Cambridge University, has questioned for many years the prioritisation of autonomy in medical law and ethics.[2] Autonomy (in the sense of individual choice) in a society where no one can be trusted would not be much good to us. We could never be sure the information we were given to make our choice could be trusted. Through her BBC Reith Lecture in 2002, Onora explains that society has created a culture of distrust.[3]

This book is a small attempt to create a culture of trust. The original title was *The Malady of Medical Law – The Disease of Distrust*. However, this seemed to further entrench distrust, which, like any disease, spreads quickly if it is given too much airtime. *Health Professionals and Trust – The Cure for Healthcare Law and Policy* suggests a more positive attitude; one that I hope this book makes infectious.

Professor Sheila McLean, Director of the Institute of Law and Ethics in Medicine, inspired this series and gave the authors the permission to take an idea and see what difference it can make.

Dr Peter Roberts, a New Zealand doctor, in his book *Snakes and Ladders: The Pursuit of a Safety Culture in New Zealand Public Hospitals*, argues that trust should be the paramount motivation for health professionals to carry out their work.[4] Dr Roberts concludes, 'Trust is the greatest deficiency [in our healthcare system]. Understanding what must be done to secure its benefit is the next quest.'[5]

Notes

1 Collins, F, *The Language of God: A Scientist Presents Evidence for Belief*, New York: Free Press, 2006.
2 O'Neill, O, *Autonomy and Trust in Bioethics*, Cambridge: Cambridge University Press, 2002.
3 O'Neill, O, *A Question of Trust*, Cambridge: Cambridge University Press, 2002.
4 Roberts, P, *Snakes and Ladders: The Pursuit of a Safety Culture in New Zealand Public Hospitals*, Wellington: Health Services Research Centre, 2003, p 110.
5 Ibid, p 153.

Chapter 1

Healthy healthcare law
depends on trust

Introduction

The idea for this book came from a comment made to me by an anaesthetist
at a medical seminar. The anaesthetist described seeing an elderly male patient
in significant pain that would be best alleviated by an epidural. The anaesthetist asked the patient if he knew what an epidural was. The patient
said, 'Yes, I have had one before, give me one now. I am in pain.' The
anaesthetist's medical instincts were to give the patient an epidural immediately; however, her fear was whether administering an epidural in these
circumstances would align with the informed consent provisions contained in
New Zealand's Code of Health and Disability Services Consumers' Rights
(Code of Consumers' Rights).[1] In actual fact, the anaesthetist could establish
adequate informed consent under the Code of Consumers' Rights because
the patient was in immediate pain, had previously had the treatment so knew
about its consequences and was requesting it right away.[2] Fortunately for the
patient, the anaesthetist, despite her apprehension about the Code of
Consumers' Rights, administered the epidural. The patient trusted the anaesthetist and ultimately the anaesthetist trusted her own medical judgment.
Both parties' trust could have been undermined by the perception that an
external piece of paper, the Code of Consumers' Rights, dictated a different
outcome.

All of the healthcare professionals at the medical seminar acknowledged
that they often felt concerned and unsure about how a particular legal guide-
line or hospital policy impacted on decisions that they made. One healthcare
professional went so far as to say that if they passed the scene of an accident,
they would think twice about stopping to help in case something went wrong
and they were held legally responsible. Trust is particularly crucial in accident
and emergency situations because these patients are often unconscious and in
serious trauma. These patients are at their most vulnerable and all they can do
is trust that healthcare professionals will make the right medical decisions to
ensure the patients' wellbeing.

Events that eroded trust

Trust is at the heart of all medical decisions. We would not ask healthcare professionals for their advice if we did not trust their expertise and judgment. The erosion of medical trust in New Zealand began with what has been called the 'unfortunate experiment'.[3] This so-called 'experiment' involved gynae-cology specialist Dr Herbert Green, who worked at National Women's Hospital in Auckland, New Zealand. Between 1966 and 1982, Dr Green carried out a study to see what would happen to women with cervical cancer symptoms if their symptoms were observed rather than treated.[4] His patients were not informed at any stage that they had symptoms of cervical cancer.[5] Some of these women died needlessly because they were systematically deprived of medical intervention that could have saved their lives.[6]

It is difficult to assess the motives behind Dr Green's actions. However, it seems Dr Green was trying to prove his personal hypothesis; that by not treating the symptoms of cervical cancer (which involved invasive treatment), his patients may not develop cervical cancer.[7] Dr Green's mistake was that he did not tell his patients what he was doing. Dr Green's patients trusted that he was doing the right thing for them, but his study was carried out on them without their informed consent. If asked, some of his patients may have chosen to follow Dr Green's hypothesis; others may well have said they would prefer the standard treatment. His patients should have been given the oppor-tunity to make these decisions about their medical treatment.

If Dr Green's hypothesis had been correct and based on the informed consent of his patients, the patients would have survived and their trust in him would have been enhanced. However, Dr Green's patients were completely betrayed because his hypothesis was wrong, the patients were not informed and their symptoms were not treated. The patients' trust in Dr Green was rightly gone.

Dr Green's actions led to a major inquiry chaired by District Court Judge Sylvia Cartwright (as she was then),[8] and the release of what has become known as the Cartwright Report.[9] The report documents an environment where healthcare professionals believed that so long as their actions would ultimately benefit patients, there was little need to communicate with patients.[10] Society had given permission for doctors to act as they thought best.[11] We had all assumed that we could trust the medical profession to do the right thing. When it turned out to be the wrong thing, an atmosphere of distrust began in New Zealand.

Similar events in the United States and United Kingdom began the erosion of trust in those countries. The Tuskegee syphilis experiment in the United States – where a number of vulnerable African–American men who had syph-ilis were not told they had syphilis, nor that penicillin could cure their afflic-tion – shows what happens when trust is abused.[12] When the trial began in 1932 in Tuskegee, Alabama, there was no known cure for syphilis.[13] The trial involved a total of 600 African–American men.[14] The United States Public Health Service diagnosed 399 of them with syphilis, but told them only that they had 'bad blood' and that their health would be monitored.[15] The monitoring would continue until they died and then an autopsy would be carried out to see the effects that syphilis had on their biological systems. A control group of 201 healthy African–American men were studied at the same time.[16] Both groups were offered free meals, transport to the clinic and a free burial.[17] When penicillin, a cure for syphilis, became available in the 1940s, the researchers did not tell the men who had syphilis about the possible treatment.[18] Many of the men, who could have been saved, died from syphilis.[19] It was not until a news media leak in 1972, 40 years after the research began, that the full implications of the research became public knowledge.[20] The healthcare professionals involved in the Tuskegee syphilis experiment prioritised their experiment, which was to observe the full effects of syphilis, over the care and wellbeing of their patients who had a condition that would certainly kill them without the available penicillin treatment.

It is difficult to think of a more gross breach of the trust that a patient is entitled to put in healthcare professionals. The patients were highly vulnerable; they were economically poor and socially disadvantaged. The free meals and transport would have been a strong incentive for them to take part. The difference in economic and social power between these men and the doctors carrying out the experiment was immense. There was no thought given to the fact that as fellow human beings, the patients were the equals of the doctors. The doctors treated them as inferiors, as a means to the ends of their research.

In 2010, the President of the United States, Barack Obama apologised to the President of Guatemala, Alvaro Colom for the Guatemalan prisoners, soldiers, prostitutes and mental patients who had been infected with sexually transmitted diseases without their knowledge.[21] Susan Reverby, a medical historian at Wellesley College in Massachusetts, unearthed the US-sponsored study that took place in Guatemala in the 1940s. The study was found in a University of Pittsburgh archive, among the papers of the United States Public Health Service researcher John Cutler.[22] Reverby discovered the records when she was researching her book about the Tuskegee experiment, *Examining Tuskegee: The Infamous Syphilis Study and its Legacy*.[23] John Cutler was also responsible for the Tuskegee research.[24] The research in Guatemala involved approximately 1,500 men and women. These people were infected with syphilis without their knowledge 'through cuts in their skin or through sex with prostitutes who had syphilis or were infected by researchers'.[25] The purpose of the study was to see whether syphilis could be prevented with penicillin, a new drug in short supply between 1946 and 1948. Seventy-one of the patients in the experiment died but, not surprisingly, the researchers were not prepared to link any of the deaths to their research.[26] The research was carried out in secret, by researchers who 'lied to their subjects and worried that the project might be "wrecked" if it became public'.[27] Reverby also describes two other abuses of power and trust as the 'trinity' of unholy medical research.[28] These involved doctors at the Jewish Chronic Disease Hospital in New York who infected patients with live cancer cells without their knowledge, and researchers who gave mentally disabled children hepatitis at Willowbrook State School without the children or the children's parents knowing.[29] The moral justification for these horrendous breaches of trust was that the 'doctors who led trials saw themselves as scientific pioneers and their patients as participants in a humanitarian mission'.[30]

Concern is expressed that the impact of Tuskegee (the most widely published experiment) is still 'breeding distrust in minorities who often are reluctant to take part in research or seek medical care'.[31] As Francis Collins, the Director of the National Institutes of Health, said, 'We are concerned about the way in which this horrendous experiment, even though it was 60 years ago, may appear to people hearing about it today.'[32] Susan Reverby rightly worries that, with so much research on drugs being carried out overseas, 'how do we keep on top of what's going on now?'[33]

In the United Kingdom, Dr Harold Shipman, who is believed to have deliberately and systematically killed over 200 of his patients, is in a similar league to the Tuskegee doctors.[34] An inquiry carried out by Dame Janet Smith found that, between 1975 and 1998, Dr Shipman killed 215 of his patients by the deliberate 'administration of a lethal dose of an opiate, most frequently diamorphine'.[35] The patients Dr Shipman killed ranged in age from 41 to 93 years old, but the majority of his victims were elderly females who lived alone.[36] Following a police investigation into the death of one of his elderly female patients in 1998, Dr Shipman was arrested and charged with murdering her and 14 of his other patients.[37] On 31 January 2000, Dr Shipman was convicted on all 15 counts of murder and sentenced to 15 terms of life imprisonment.[38] Following the criminal trial, 'the Director of Public Prosecutions announced that no further criminal proceedings would be instituted against Shipman'.[39] The Secretary of State for Health, following resolutions from both Houses of Parliament, established the Shipman Inquiry on 31 January 2001.[40] This inquiry established the full extent of Dr Shipman's horrific behaviour, which the earlier police investigation had only hinted at.

Dr Shipman's patients trusted him as a medical practitioner, and he grossly abused that trust by taking their lives. However, the betrayal of trust goes much deeper than this. As Dame Janet Smith explains:

> Deeply shocking though it is, the bare statement that Shipman has killed over 200 patients does not fully reflect the enormity of his crimes. As a general practitioner, Shipman was trusted implicitly by his patients and their families. He betrayed their trust in a way and to an extent that I believe is unparalleled in history ... Although I have identified 215 victims of Shipman, the true number is far greater and cannot be counted. I include the thousands of relatives, friends and neighbours who have lost

a loved one or a friend before his or her time, in circumstances which will leave their mark for ever . . . There are also the hundreds of patients of Shipman who have been deeply disturbed by the realisation that Shipman was not the kind, caring and sympathetic man they took him for. They too must feel betrayed. Shipman has also damaged the good name of the medical profession and has caused many patients to doubt whether they can trust their own family doctor. This trust forms the basis of the relationship between doctor and patient. Although I believe that the overwhelming majority of patients will, on reflection, realise that they can indeed trust their doctor as they always have done, there will be some who will remain uncertain.[41]

In all of the above abuses of trust, there was a major power imbalance between the patients and the healthcare professionals. In the Tuskegee study, the men were all poor, illiterate, socially marginalised and discriminated against. In the Guatemalan prisoners study, the men were vulnerable because they were in prison. Dr Shipman's patients were all elderly, living alone and socially isolated. These groups were utterly at the mercy of what they were told by their doctors. Their trust – that no harm was being done to them – was brutally abused.

Ian Kennedy, in his book *The Unmasking of Medicine*,[42] and Ivan Illich, in his book *Limits to Medicine*,[43] illustrate the significant power that medical professionals wield in society because they literally hold life and death in their hands. The medical profession defines what good and bad health is and determines when a life is beyond saving. Medical professionals are given access to our most intimate selves. They decide which drugs may help us. Kennedy and Illich ask us to question whether we can trust a profession with so much power. Kennedy suggests, 'we must challenge the power which doctors exert over our lives'.[44] Illich says, 'Society has transferred to physicians the exclusive right to determine what constitutes sickness, who is or might become sick and what should be done to such people.'[45] These seminal books rightly show the frightening amount of power healthcare professionals have because of the nature of their work, and note the ever-present potential for that power to be misused.

The idea of marketplace competition swept through the Western world in the late 1980s and early 1990s.[46] Competition was seen as the way to make professions maximally productive and to drive down prices. In New Zealand, for example, Parliament even contemplated opening up the dental profession to the marketplace.[47] The assumption was that the public would work out, through a competitive market, which dentists were worth going to; that way, those who were incompetent or without adequate qualifications would go out of business.[48]

In the United States, David Rogers, the Welsh McDermott University Professor of Medicine at Cornell University Medical College, wrote, 'Nothing has done more damage to the "trust" part of medicine than the belief that the use of marketplace ethics and competition would improve medicine or make it less expensive.'[49] Rogers quotes the satiric American health economist, Uwe Reinhardt, who said that competition, when stripped of all its niceties, means 'I'm going to try and drive you out of business'.[50] Rogers is bewildered by how many physicians in the United States have taken up the philosophy of competition.[51] For Rogers, 'co-operation, concerns with feelings, needs and the sensitivities of one's fellow man should be paramount' in the medical profession, and competition directly undermines these values.[52] In the United States, Rogers states that the choice was between economic autonomy (where there are no restrictions on personal income or resources devoted to medicine) and professional autonomy and that, ultimately, economic autonomy was the victor.[53] With increasing regulation and supervision of healthcare professionals' actions, Rogers believes that it is 'little wonder, as government and insurance companies supervised doctors more, and trusted them less, patient trust was one of the factors to suffer profoundly'.[54]

The further undermining of trust by audit

If we believe healthcare professionals cannot be trusted, then monitoring processes are assumed to restore trust. Michael Power, in his book, *The Audit Explosion*, which primarily focuses on financial audits, points out that the assumption behind the growth of such audits was an 'erosion of trust'.[55] As Power states, 'It came to be accepted that actions could no longer be co-ordinated by trust and that instead independent "outsiders" had to be used to restore that trust by providing *ex post* validations of auditee performance.'[56] Power suggests a similar view to that which will be pursued in this book, saying, 'audit has spread as much because of its power as an idea, and that contrary to the assumptions of the story of lost trust, its spread actually creates the very distrust it is meant to address'.[57] Power believes that people 'may adapt their behaviour to reflect the fact that they are not trusted and thereby confirm that they should not be trusted'.[58] Diego Gambetta confirms this analysis in his book on trust.[59] The more people are distrusted, the more untrustworthy they are likely to become. Rogers says 'if one fundamentally believes that human beings are basically lazy, that they require goads, fear of punishment, and strict and explicit ground rules to do the right thing', then not surprisingly, human beings governed by those who hold such a philosophy 'quite predictably behave in ways that reinforce this sour view of mankind'.[60] Not only does external audit reinforce that the person audited cannot be trusted, it also creates a culture of compliance for compliance sake rather than for the good of the patient. As Power points out, 'Concepts of performance and quality are in danger of being defined largely in terms of conformity to auditable process. Indeed, the construction of auditable environments has necessitated record-keeping demands, which only serve the audit process.'[61]

The preoccupation is with the 'auditable process rather than the substance of the activities'.[62] A culture of compliance replaces what should be open and honest dialogue between medical peers and their patients as to how they can ensure they are delivering the best possible healthcare service to their patients. This should be done in the 'spirit of reflective self-improvement'.[63] Audit is based on the assumption that we cannot trust professionals. Instead, we have to watch over them. How then can we trust those who carry out the audit process? Enron has shown that when the culture is one of self-interest, auditors themselves buy into that culture and cannot be trusted.[64] Once there is a culture of self-interest and distrust, audit makes no difference.

The public still have trust

Popular perception shows that, notwithstanding the misdeeds of some physicians, healthcare professionals are ranked highly by the public in opinion polls. The polls do not tell us why healthcare professionals rate well for trust, or even what those who fill out the polls mean by trust. Such polls are, instead, a general measure of public perception across a range of professions. *The Reader's Digest* commissioned an independent research firm, The Leading Edge, to survey 500 adults in New Zealand,[65] and 750 adults in Australia.[66] Survey participants were asked, amongst other things, to rate on a scale of 1 to 10 how much they trusted different professions. In the 2008 New Zealand Reader's Digest Survey, ambulance officers were rated as the second most trusted profession behind fire fighters.[67] Pilots were third on the list ahead of nurses (fourth), doctors (fifth), pharmacists (sixth), veterinarians (seventh) and dentists (11th equal with police officers).[68] Chief Executive Officers (CEOs; those in charge of healthcare operations and subject to external control) were 30th on the list.[69] In the Australian Reader's Digest Survey, ambulance officers were rated the most trustworthy profession ahead of fire fighters.[70] Pilots came in third on the list ahead of nurses (fourth), pharmacists (fifth), doctors (sixth), veterinarians (seventh) and dentists (12th).[71] CEOs were well down the list in 33rd place.[72] Lawyers, who are part of most ethics committees and disciplinary tribunals, were only the 28th most trusted profession in New Zealand,[73] and the 31st in Australia.[74]

The Royal College of Physicians commissioned the Ipsos MORI Social Research Institute to carry out such polls in the United Kingdom.[75] In 2009 the sample was of 2,023 15-year-olds and over across Great Britain.[76] The first question asked was who you trust to tell the truth. Doctors came in at the top of the list with 92 per cent of those surveyed believing they tell the truth ahead of teachers (88 per cent), and professors and judges (80 per cent) ahead of clergy and priests.[77] Doctors have topped the poll since the surveys began in 1983.[78] Overall trends indicate that trust in most professions has declined, except for judges, in whom trust has increased.[79]

The Royal College of Physicians survey shows some interesting differences about who trusts whom. When ethnicity is taken into account, results indicate that Caucasians are more likely than ethnic minority communities to trust professions.[80] Those in regular employment have greater trust in professions than those who are not.[81] These findings are consistent with the work of Melissa Ahern and Michael Hendryx, who carried out an extensive study to identify sources of trust in characteristics of healthcare systems and the wider community.[82] What the authors call 'social capital' – communities where there are shared norms and shared activities – influences the level of trust people perceive in healthcare professionals.[83] We trust those who seem most like ourselves.

Why trust is crucial

In the chapter entitled 'Ethics and Patient Rights' in the *Report of the Cervical Cancer Inquiry 1988*, Judge Sylvia Cartwright said that:

> A patient who enters hospital for examination or treatment will usually be nervous and feel out of her depth. She may be surprised by how little information is offered about her diagnosis and management. Frequently she will ask very few questions of the nursing or medical staff. Occasionally, she will be outraged when she learns that treatment or procedures have been undertaken without her knowledge or consent. Overwhelmingly, however, she will trust the medical, nursing and administrative staff to have one overriding goal: her health and welfare.[84]

As Onora O'Neill eloquently says:

> Each of us and every profession and every institution needs trust. We need it because we have to be able to rely on others acting as they say that they will, and because we need others to accept that we will act as we say we will.[85]

O'Neill goes on to quote sociologist Niklas Luhmann, who states succinctly, 'A complete absence of trust would prevent [one] even from getting up in the morning.'[86] Whenever we are ill, we rely on healthcare professionals to tell us the right things, to listen to and understand our symptoms and to react quickly and correctly if the situation is urgent. We have no option but to trust them. As Onora O'Neill points out, informed consent, which for our purposes is meant to empower patients, 'presupposes and expresses trust'.[87] I have to rely on the surgeon to explain the operation to me before I can make my informed choice. I have to work out for myself whether I can place trust in the particular surgeon. Anything that makes it difficult to know when to place that trust in the healthcare professional puts the patient at risk. The more complex the layers of scrutiny, the more likely healthcare professionals and patients are to become confused and unsure.

A debate between internal and external regulation, between virtue ethics (which places the focus on the individual to be a good citizen) and external ethics (which places the focus on external principles to create good behaviour) misses a crucial point. Whether you call it internal or external regulation, ultimately both forms of regulation involve people with their own myriad of vested interests. External regulation is no more objective than internal regulation. Enron shows us that once greed and vested interests set in, neither internal nor external regulation will make any difference whatsoever.[88]

In fact, the existence of external regulation, with its appearance of neutrality, is more likely to mislead us and lead to a false sense of security. Auditing does not in itself create trust. It must come from internal responsibility and a commitment to be trustworthy. It must come from a profession's desire to be trustworthy and to be constantly vigilant within its own ranks to any behaviour that would undermine that trust. Trust cannot be created by a paper trail. It can only exist in the hearts, minds and behaviours of people. This was recognised as far back as 1974 when the then Medical Superintendent-in-Chief set out guidelines for the introduction of ethical committees to Auckland Hospital Board institutions. The second 'guiding principle' reads, 'In the long run no law or code, however detailed, can be a substitute for basically what is a trust between the medical profession and society, between the patient and the doctor.'[89]

Philip Zimbardo conducted an experiment at Stanford University where some participants were asked to play the role of prison guards and the other participants were prison inmates.[90] The two-week experiment had to be stopped after just six days because those playing the guards began to seriously abuse the inmates, both psychologically and physically.[91] Zimbardo believes we are all capable of being drawn into bad behaviour because human behaviour is determined more by situational forces and group dynamics than by anything inherent in our nature.[92] Peer pressure to do the right thing is more powerful than an external ethics committee setting out guidelines for behaviour.

Jay Katz, a physician who spent most of his professional life teaching at Yale Law School, traces what he calls the history of silence between healthcare professionals and patients in his book, *The Silent World of Doctor and Patient*.[93] Hippocrates, the archangel of ethics for healthcare professionals, said, 'The physician must be ready, not only to do his duty himself, but also to secure the co-operation of the patient, of the attendants and of externals.'[94] The physician is portrayed by Hippocrates as a 'cheerful' and 'serene'[95] person who diverts the patient's attention away from what was being done to them by a variety of methods – either 'sharply' or 'emphatically',[96] or with 'solicitude' and 'attention'.[97] The assumption was that the healthcare professional would act in the best interests of the patient and the patient would obey the healthcare professional. The healthcare professional and the patient were assumed to have the common goal of recovery and care. They were united through the idea of *philia*, the Greek word for friendship. As Plato explains, the sick man loves a physician merely because he is sick.[98] At the heart of this friendship is implicit trust that the healthcare professional will do the right thing and will do what is necessary to make the patient better. Who of us, when we are really sick, would not want healthcare professionals to take over and make us better? As Katz finds in his historical analysis of Western medicine, 'The history of the physician–patient relationship from ancient times to the present bears testimony to physicians' caring dedication to their patients' physical welfare.'[99]

Rogers maintains:

> that our only excuse for taking 4–10 years of a young person's life in order to make him or her a doctor is to build into their souls an absolutely sacred feeling of responsibility for patient welfare which will serve as their unswerving internal compass for the remainder of their lives.[100]

We know such trust can be abused, just as the trust we give to parents to provide for the best interests of their children is sometimes misplaced.[101] We must find ways to foster trust between patients and healthcare professionals with the knowledge that there is always potential for it to be sabotaged.

Why do we trust or not?

The trends in the opinion polls analysed above are worth thinking about. Generally, across all the polls, the more at risk we are – in cases of fire and emergency, for example – the higher the level of trust we have for those professions who come to the rescue. These results may be based on participants' past experiences, or because there are few examples of abuses of trust in these situations, or it may be that because people are so vulnerable in such situations, trust is particularly important to them. It may also be that in those high-risk situations, the professionals involved have to put their own needs second, drop everything and attend to the immediate needs of others. We innately admire and trust people who can do this. There is a sharing of vulnerability: the patient is at risk and the emergency professionals place themselves at risk to save the patient.

It is the most vulnerable, those in minority ethnic groups and those who are not in paid work who feel the least trust for professions. There is the biggest power differential between these groups and healthcare professionals. This could lead to some professionals treating people differently depending on their ethnic and social class, and those groups feeling less respected, understood and listened to. It could be because many in those groups do not have easy access to professionals and what they do not know, they do not trust.

Whatever the reasons for the differences between who is generally trusted by whom, there is a strong connection between vulnerability and trust, whether it be the vulnerability of the emergency situation or ethnic and social vulnerability. It is also extremely clear that those who 'manage' healthcare, such as CEOs, are far less trusted than frontline healthcare professionals such as ambulance workers, nurses and doctors. Lawyers, who prosecute, protect and defend healthcare workers when things go wrong, are far less trusted than the frontline healthcare professionals themselves.

The surveys do not tell us what trust is, nor how to foster and nurture trust. The surveys also do not explain how trust is undermined and potentially destroyed. This book uses philosophical arguments to describe what trust is and how best to enhance it. Trust is most likely to thrive where there is an inner desire and responsibility to act in a trustworthy manner. Economists say that there need to be incentives to create that inner desire. External regulation and surveillance may, at best, lead to compliance, but this compliance is not likely to be as enduring as a professional commitment to act in trustworthy ways. Healthcare professionals must either develop a strong professional commitment to creating a culture of trust, or face more and more external audits. If that is not incentive enough, then nothing is.

This book is written for patients, healthcare professionals and those who decide and apply health law, namely politicians, judges, tribunals and managers. It is written at a time when trust is a sparse commodity, in a world where politics and religion divide many people and global capitalism dominates the economy of the world.[102] It is also written at a time when the gap between the so-called first and third worlds is large.[103] Technology continues to advance, leading to new treatment, more choice and more complexity. Healthcare professionals range from those working in war zones with limited resources,[104] or working in tsunami-devastated conditions,[105] fire-devastated conditions,[106] or the annihilation after a major earthquake,[107] to those working in five-star hospitals with the most modern drugs and every available piece of diagnostic equipment. In all the above situations, the patients have to trust healthcare professionals to give them the best possible healthcare in the circumstances. A compliance committee leaning over the shoulder of all the healthcare professionals would not have led to better decisions. The compliance committees may well just get in the way of the work that needs to be done. The resources necessary to have compliance committees present are better spent providing medical support at the scene of the treatment.

Of even greater concern is that there is no guarantee that compliance committees will make healthcare professionals more trustworthy. Members of compliance committees are human beings, just like the healthcare professionals. They can get things wrong, they can let their judgments be diverted or distracted by irrelevant matters, by personal bias, by likes and dislikes, by the emotions they are feeling. As O'Neill says, it is an 'unrealistic hankering for a world in which safety and compliance are total, and breaches of trust are totally eliminated'.[108] O'Neill suggests that the 'culture of accountability that we are relentlessly building for ourselves actually damages trust rather than supporting it'.[109] External controls are brought in because internal controls are not trusted. The more external controls there are, the less trust there is in internal controls. Taken to its logical conclusion, total external control will destroy internal trust. O'Neill is right, it is time to take stock and look to other, better ways of preserving and strengthening a trustworthy healthcare profession.

In the Cartwright Report, Dame Cartwright herself concluded in 'Ethics and Patient Rights' that she preferred to:

> advocate a system which will encourage better communication between patient and doctor, allow for structured negotiation and mediation, and raise awareness of patients' medical, cultural and family needs. The focus of attention must shift from the doctor to the patient.[110]

Good communication between healthcare professional and patient is essential for trust to develop. Good communication means the health professional must really listen to their patient. This includes listening to what the patient says, how the patient feels and also taking account of the patient's symptoms. It means the healthcare professional must explain things and ask questions in a way the patient can understand, and respond to appropriately. The patient must have confidence that they can tell the healthcare professional what they are really going through and that they will be listened to. The healthcare professional must be up to date in their knowledge and sharp in their diagnostic skills so they can give advice that is relevant to the particular patient. The shift of attention to the patient has, in reality, been a shift to external controls of the relationship, such as health commissioners and ethics committees. The focus must go back to the relationship between patients and healthcare professionals. If patients cannot trust healthcare professionals, then codes of patients' rights become meaningless. As Richard Holton says, 'When you trust someone to do something, you rely on them to do it, and you regard that reliance in a certain way: you have a readiness to feel betrayal should it be disappointed, and gratitude should it be upheld.'[111] Rights are only effective if those who have the duty to act on them can be trusted to do so. Trust is the primary value for the relationship between patient and healthcare professional to work. The purpose of healthcare law and policy must be to establish an environment in which trust thrives.

Notes

1 Code of Health and Disability Services Consumers' Rights as prescribed by the Health and Disability Commissioner (Code of Health and Disability Services Consumers' Rights) Regulations 1996.
2 Right 7(1) of the Code of Health and Disability Services Consumers' Rights. For an introductory discussion of informed consent in New Zealand see Skegg, P, 'Consent to Treatment: Introduction', in Skegg, P and Paterson, R (eds), *Medical Law in New Zealand*, Wellington: Brookers Ltd, 2006, pp 145–169.
3 Coney, S and Bunkle, P, 'An "Unfortunate Experiment" at National Women's', *Metro*, June 1987.
4 Ibid.
5 Ibid, pp 51–52.
6 Ibid, p 53.

7   Ibid, p 50.
8   In 1993 Dame Sylvia Cartwright became the first woman in New Zealand to be appointed to the High Court. Dame Sylvia Cartwright was also the New Zealand Governor General between 2001 and 2006. Clark, H, 'PM Welcomes Governor-General-Designate', *beehive.govt.nz*, 24 August 2000.
9   Cartwright, S, *The Report of the Cervical Cancer Inquiry 1988*, Auckland: Government Printing Office, 1988.
10 Ibid, p 215.
11 There is still ongoing debate as to how wrong Dr Green's actions and motives were. See generally Bryer, L, *A History of the 'Unfortunate Experiment' at National Women's Hospital*, Auckland: Auckland University Press, 2009.
12 Jones, J, *Bad Blood: The Tuskegee Experiment*, New York: The Free Press, 1981.
13 Ibid, p 1.
14 Ibid.
15 Ibid, pp 1, 5–6.
16 Ibid, p 1.
17 Ibid, p 4.
18 Ibid, pp 8–9.
19 As at 1969, between 28 and 100 people had died as a direct result of complications caused by syphilis. Still others 'developed serious syphilis-related heart conditions that may have contributed to their deaths.' Ibid, p 2.
20 Heller, J, 'Syphilis Victims in the US Study Went Untreated for 40 Years', *New York Times*, 26 July 1972.
21 Sternberg, S, 'Revelation a Reminder of Era of Abuse', *Otago Daily Times World Focus*, 4–10 October 2010, p 8.
22 Ibid.
23 Reverby, S, *Examining Tuskegee: The Infamous Syphilis Study and its Legacy*, Chapel Hill: The University of North Carolina Press, 2009.
24 Op. cit., Sternberg, p 8.
25 Ibid.
26 Ibid.
27 Ibid.
28 Ibid.
29 Ibid.
30 Ibid.
31 Ibid.
32 Ibid.
33 Ibid.
34 Smith, J, *The Shipman Inquiry Volume 1: Death Disguised*, Manchester: The Shipman Inquiry, 2002. See also, Dyer, C, 'GP Faces 15 Charges of Murder', *British Medical Journal* 319, 1999, p 938.
35 Op. cit., Smith, p 2.
36 Ibid, pp 2–3.
37 Ibid, p 1.
38 Ibid.
39 Ibid.
40 Ibid, p 2.
41 Ibid, pp 201–202.
42 Kennedy, I, *The Unmasking of Medicine*, London: George Allen and Unwin, 1981.
43 Illich, I, *Limits to Medicine: Medical Nemesis, the Expropriation of Health*, London: Marion Boyars, 1976.
44 Op. cit., Kennedy, p 167.
45 Op. cit., Illich, p 6.

46 See generally, Friedman, M, *Capitalism and Freedom*, Chicago: University of Chicago Press, 1962.
47 See the Parliamentary debates over the passage of the Dental Act 1988, for example (8 December 1987) 485 NZPD 1619, pp 1619–1627.
48 Ibid, p 1624.
49 Rogers, D, 'On Trust: A Basic Building Block For Healing Doctor-Patient Interactions', *Journal of the Royal Society of Medicine* 87, 1994, p 3.
50 Ibid.
51 Ibid.
52 Ibid.
53 Ibid.
54 Ibid.
55 Power, M, *The Audit Explosion*, London: Demos, 1996, p 12.
56 Ibid.
57 Ibid, p 13.
58 Ibid.
59 Gambetta, D (ed.), *Trust: Making and Breaking Cooperative Relations*, New York: Blackwell Publishers, 1990.
60 Op. cit., Rogers, p 4.
61 Op. cit., Power, p 48.
62 Ibid.
63 Pollitt, C, 'The Struggle for Quality: The Case of the National Health Service', *Policy and Politics* 21, 1993, p 168.
64 See generally, Sauviat, C, 'The Demise of Andersen: A Consequence of Corporate Governance Failure in the Context of Major Changes in the Accounting Profession and the Audit Market', in Dembinski, P *et al* (eds), *Enron and World Finance: A Case Study in Ethics*, New York: Palgrave MacMillan, 2006; Travis, A, 'Enron *et al.* and Implications for the Auditing Profession', in Dembinski, P *et al* (eds), *Enron and World Finance: A Case Study in Ethics*, New York: Palgrave MacMillan, 2006; Blommestein, H, 'How to Restore Trust in Financial Markets?', in Dembinski, P *et al* (eds), *Enron and World Finance: A Case Study in Ethics*, New York: Palgrave MacMillan, 2006; and Reiter, S and Williams, P, 'The Philosophy and Rhetoric of Auditor Independence Concepts', *Business Ethics Quarterly* 14, 2004, pp 355–376.
65 The Leading Edge, '2008 New Zealand's Most Trusted Professions', *Reader's Digest Magazine*, 2008.
66 The Leading Edge, 'Australia's Most Trusted Professions 2008', *Reader's Digest Magazine*, 2008.
67 Op. cit., The Leading Edge, '2008 New Zealand's Most Trusted Professions'.
68 Ibid.
69 Ibid.
70 Op. cit., The Leading Edge, 'Australia's Most Trusted Professions 2008'.
71 Ibid.
72 Ibid.
73 Op. cit., The Leading Edge, '2008 New Zealand's Most Trusted Professions'.
74 Op. cit., The Leading Edge, 'Australia's Most Trusted Professions 2008'.
75 Royal College of Physicians, *Trust in Doctors 2009: Annual Survey of Public Trust in Professions*, London: Ipsos MORI, 2009.
76 Ibid, p 1.
77 Ibid, p 4.
78 Ibid, p 3.
79 Ibid, p 7.

80 Ibid, p 8.
81 Ibid.
82 Ahern, M and Hendryx, M, 'Social Capital and Trust in Providers', *Social Sciences and Medicine* 57, 2003, pp 1195–1203.
83 Ibid, p 1195.
84 Op. cit., Cartwright, p 127.
85 O'Neill, O, *A Question of Trust: The BBC Reith Lectures 2002*, Cambridge: Cambridge University Press, 2002, pp 3–4.
86 Luhmann, N, *Trust and Power*, Chichester: John Wiley & Sons, 1979, p 4.
87 Op. cit., O'Neill, p 87.
88 See generally, op. cit., Sauviat; op. cit., Travis; op. cit., Blommestein; and op.cit., Reiter and Williams.
89 Op. cit., Cartwright, p 143.
90 Zimbardo, P, *The Lucifer Effect: Understanding How Good People Turn Evil*, New York: Random House, 2007.
91 Ibid, pp 154–180.
92 Ibid, pp 3–22.
93 Katz, J, *The Silent World of Doctor and Patient*, New York: Free Press, 1984.
94 Hippocrates, 'Aphorisms', in Jones, W (trans.), *Hippocrates Volume IV*, Cambridge: Harvard University Press, 1953, p 99.
95 Hippocrates, 'Decorum', in Jones, W (trans.), *Hippocrates Volume II*, Cambridge: Harvard University Press, 1952, p 297.
96 Ibid.
97 Ibid, p 299.
98 Plato, 'Lysis', in Hamilton, E and Cairns, H (eds), *The Collected Dialogues of Plato*, Princeton: Princeton University Press, 1961, p. 162.
99 Katz, op cit., p. 28.
100 Rogers, op. cit., p. 4.
101 See generally, Freeman, M, *The Rights and Wrongs of Children*, London: F. Pinter, 1983.
102 Gray, J, *False Dawn: The Delusions of Global Capitalism*, London: Granta Publications, 1998, shows that capitalism, United States style, will not lead to the utopia of a single, super-efficient global market, but more likely to a kind of permanent anarchy.
103 See generally, Sachs, J, *Common Wealth: Economics for a Crowded Planet*, London: Penguin Books, 2009, which provides a plan for the future.
104 Maier, M, 'Afghan Security Forces Gain 52 New Doctors and Nurses', *NATO Training Mission-Afghanistan*, 18 April 2010; 'SAF Team in Afghanistan', *The Straits Times*, 2 April 2010.
105 'Samoa Hospital Sees Post-Tsunami Sanitation and Food-Related Illness', *Radio New Zealand*, 7 October 2009; 'Hospital Arrives in Aceh as Logjam Delays Aid', *The Sydney Morning Herald*, 8 January 2005.
106 'Bushfire Doctor Shows Value of Locum Work', *Rural Healthcare Australia*, 2009.
107 Couric, K, 'Haiti's 21st Century Makeshift Hospital', *CBS News*, 23 April 2010; Permatasari, S and Sukarsono, A, 'Indonesian Doctors Struggle as Quake Death Toll Rises', *Bloomberg Press*, 2 October 2009.
108 Op. cit., O'Neill, p 19.
109 Ibid.
110 Op. cit., Cartwright, p 176.
111 Holton, R, 'Deciding to Trust, Coming to Believe', *Australasian Journal of Philosophy* 72, 1994, p 67.

Chapter 2

What is trust?

Subjectivity of trust

Annette Baier, in her work *Moral Prejudices*, says, 'When I trust another, I depend on her goodwill toward me.'[1] As a consequence, 'Trust . . . is accepted vulnerability to another's possible but not expected ill will (or lack of good-will) toward one.'[2] There is inevitably an element of subjectivity to trust. The truster and the trusted may well have different views on what goodwill is. The truster may have very high expectations of what should happen, whereas the trusted may have a lower standard in mind. Expectations are relevant to the sphere of influence for which trust is given. For example, when I am on holiday I trust you to live in my house and look after it by keeping it clean and tidy. That trust does not extend as far as giving you permission to rear-range all the rooms in my house and to paint the interior ceilings every colour of the rainbow. Often, expectations about the standard and sphere of trust are assumed on the basis of shared social norms or past experience. When the assumption is misread and there is no other communication to clarify it, then trust will break down. For example, the healthcare professional assumes it is acceptable for the patient to be left on a bed in the corridor because that is what happens when the hospital is busy. The patient, on the other hand, may never have been to a hospital before and feel acutely embarrassed about being in a corridor with numerous strangers going past. The patient may begin to distrust those carrying out the treatment.

A key to building an environment of trust is to clearly and accurately communicate what one's expectations are. Even if nothing is being said, expectations are forming. The expectations may be in sync or they may be miles apart. The patient may think the doctor is going to make them better straight away. However, the doctor may decide that the patient's treatment requires a long-term programme of lifestyle changes as well as medical care before their health improves. Trust can only thrive when healthcare profes-sionals and patients are clear about their expectations of likely outcomes and agree as to who will do what in the relationship. For example, the healthcare professional will prescribe a treatment plan that the patient understands and that is manageable, while the patient will let the healthcare professional know if there are unforseen difficulties in carrying through the arrangements.

Trust and risk

The discretionary elements of trust mean that trust always entails risk. As David Hume, in his *Treatise on Human Nature*, said, ' 'Tis impossible to separate [the chance of] good from the [risk of] ill.'[3] The discretionary elements of trust are compounded in the healthcare professional/patient relationship. Very sick patients, very young patients, those who do not speak the language or understand the culture, and elderly patients with Alzheimer's disease are not always in a position to clarify their expectations – they are totally vulnerable to the goodwill of their carers.

Baier argues that trust 'is reliance on others' competence and willingness to look after, rather than harm, things one cares about which are entrusted to their care'.[4] Baier proposes a test whereby trust is 'morally decent' when the continuation of the trust relationship 'need not rely on successful threats held over the trusted or on her successful cover-up of breaches of trust'.[5] Baier goes on to say that to be 'morally decent' a trust relationship must be 'able to survive awareness by each party to the relationship of *what* the other relies on in the first to ensure their continued trustworthiness or trustingness'.[6] Accordingly, Baier explains that a 'trust relationship is morally bad to the extent that either party relies on qualities in the other which would be weakened by the knowledge that the other relies on them'.[7] If a healthcare professional can only be trusted to do the right thing because of a fear of repercussions if they do not, the trust relationship is potentially unstable. In these circumstances, the trusted person is only trusted because of a particular weakness, namely fear of consequences, and is therefore likely to try to cover up their weakness.[8] This increases the potential for the trusted person to cover up breaches of trust because the truster is not aware of them, or to persuade the truster to forgive any breach by relying on their good nature. Over time, once there is knowledge of cover-up and repeated reliance on the good nature of the truster, this is likely to lead to breakdown of the trust, depending on the patience of the truster. Not many people would like to think that their healthcare professional would only treat them properly because they were worried about external repercussions if they did not. That would be a relationship of fear rather than one of trust. No one can live or work in fear for long periods. It saps human spirit and initiative.

In a ideal moral world, a trust relationship:

> Where each relies on the other's love, concern for some common good, or professional pride in competent discharge of responsibility, knowledge of what the other is relying on in one need not undermine but will more likely strengthen those relied-on features.[9]

If we know a healthcare professional really cares about us, and is scrupulous about their professional responsibilities to do the best they can for each patient, we will trust that person.

Baier accepts that what are seen as offensive forms of reliance will vary from context to context and from individual to individual.[10] Some patients may not care whether it is fear or pride in competence that motivates trust in healthcare professionals, as long as the outcome is favourable and the treatment appropriate. The Hippocratic oath to 'first do no harm' creates a climate of goodwill rather than ill will.[11] The patient does not want to be harmed. In that sense, the Hippocratic oath ensures that the interests of healthcare professionals and patients are congruent. Healthcare professionals have their own internal interests in taking the patients' interests into account. Russell Hardin, in his work *Trust and Trustworthiness*, conceptualises trust as encapsulated interests; literally, 'I trust you because your interest encapsulates mine, which is to say that you have an interest in fulfilling my trust.'[12] Hardin puts a particular emphasis on wanting the relationship to continue.[13] This reflects a common traditional practice whereby each family used to have a family doctor who was totally trusted and this relationship often continued through more than one generation of the family. The healthcare professionals and patients' interests were deeply intertwined. The wonderful television series *Dr Finlay's Casebook* captured this era.[14] There were no ethics committees, performance indicators, Codes of Rights or Health Commissioners in sight. All his patients trusted Doctor Finlay, and he trusted them. All worked together for the good health of the community. Such nirvanas of healthcare practice may still exist in small rural communities, but they are much more the exception rather than the rule in today's healthcare world.

Trust and systems

Patients are more likely to be treated by a system rather than an individual when they go into hospital. I have vivid experience of this based on the illness of a family member.[15] Three different nurses took my family member's pulse and details. There was then a considerable wait until a medical registrar asked a few questions. Another wait took place in a corridor where, ironically, there was a Code of Consumers' Rights on the wall. The family member joked that it did not mean anything to them; all they wanted was for someone to remove their pain. After three hours of waiting, another doctor decided that my family member would be taken into a ward, where they were dealt with by a number of nurses and doctors. Various X-rays were taken. The diagnosis was incomplete in the sense that the cause of the severe soreness in the stomach was not fully understood, but the pain did subside and we were allowed to go home.

What struck me was how all the healthcare professionals only saw little snippets of what was happening. There was no time for any one of them to fully understand the patient. They were all very pleasant, but they were driven by a time-and-process clock. They were all highly professional and all had goodwill toward the patient. No doubt notes were taken on a chart and test results entered into the healthcare system. As an observer, I felt the family member was being treated by a system rather than by a healthcare professional. It was difficult for me, and the family member, to trust any of the healthcare professionals' judgments. Efficiency is important in a healthcare system, but it has the potential to undermine the communication needed to build up a relationship of trust.

Raymond Tallis, in his book *Hippocratic Oaths: Medicine and Its Discontents*, argues that rather than consultants being 'god-like' in the hospital system, they are much more 'cog-like'.[16] Tallis describes the consultant thus:

> Her ward rounds are carried out faster than she finds comfortable; overbooked, under-resourced clinics are "got through" at a speed incompatible with giving patients the time and attention they need and the consultant would like to give them; the endless paperwork is disposed of at a gallop; teaching is squeezed in; reading journals to keep up to date is snatched along with lunch.[17]

Tallis cites a study showing that consultants spend only half as much time in consultation with patients as they did in 1988.[18] The study concluded that the hours spent in outpatients (patients coming into hospital for a specific treatment on the day) by doctors were lengthening because of non-clinical work such as administration duties, phone-call interruptions and looking for missing case notes.[19] The time healthcare professionals spend with patients is shortening. This struck a chord with me as I sat with my family member in the corridor of the emergency department, watching a number of healthcare professionals looking at computer screens. I wondered what they were doing; no doubt they were carrying out administration duties and possibly looking for case notes. The consultant is caught like a cog in the system. The patient has no choice but to submit to and ultimately trust a system that they do not understand and that is generally not explained to them.

Victoria McEvoy, an assistant professor of paediatrics at Harvard Medical School argues, in an article in the Harvard Medical Alumni Bulletin, that only those with 'superhuman-type' powers can survive in the healthcare world:

> Docs of Steel! Faster than a speeding bullet, yet with no stone left unturned. Paperwork? Bring it on! There is no problem too obscure, no ailment we cannot Google. As we draw our capes around us and prepare to plunge into the next pit of human suffering, we pause only to check schedules, to ensure that productivity remains on target. Juggling BlackBerries, cell phones, electronic medical records, notes from specialists, lab results, patient phone calls, referrals, radiology requests, beepers, handheld formularies, patient-satisfaction surveys, color-coded preferred-drug charts from insurers, and quality report cards from HMOs, we forge on, as our patients wait,

shivering expectantly . . . the superhuman demands of our speciality have either morphed us into steely-eyed combatants or reduced us to blithering, overwhelmed, white-coated globs of jelly. We now practice triage medicine – surrendering time-honoured bedside roles to hospitalists; slicing face time with patients; retreating to administrative roles; appending MBA, Esq., or MPH to our names to shield us from the line of fire.[20]

Adam Seligman, in his work *The Problem of Trust*, traces an evolution of Western society from pre-modern conditions in which group sanctions rather than trust was the basis of group life.[21] In modern society, the emergence of the individual meant that trust became the unifying factor of civil society. In more recent times, as Seligman explains, 'the rule-bound behavior of system confidence' takes over.[22] Matters are taken out of our hands by the system. This became clear to me when my family member was in hospital. I suggested to a nurse that more fluids were needed and that some sugar in the fluids may help. The nurse said that was for a doctor to decide and that nothing could be done until the doctor came and approved it. Fortunately, a more experienced nurse of what may be called 'the old school variety' could see for herself that the patient was dehydrated and needed sugar so went ahead and added more fluid and sugar to the drip. This made a big difference to the patient's wellbeing. This nurse's actions reminded me of the television series *House*, where Dr House does not follow the system but makes his own judgment as to the right thing to do.[23]

Systems have their place; without them, there would be chaos. We have so many systems nowadays, ranging from management systems and disciplinary systems through to professional systems, that it is very easy for the key individuals – the healthcare professional and the patient – to become lost. Trust, as the basis for the relationship between healthcare professional and patient, is being replaced by the rules, practices and processes of systems. Yet those rules, practices and processes cannot do the thinking and problem solving necessary to diagnose and treat a particular patient. That judgment is an art, a human skill exercised in the moment, which the patient has to trust. Jerome Groopman, in his book *How Doctors Think*, says: 'Different doctors . . . achieve competency in remarkably similar ways, despite working in disparate fields. Primarily, they recognize and remember their mistakes and misjudgements, and incorporate those memories into their thinking.'[24]

Healthcare professionals need to be open about their mistakes and share these with other healthcare professionals and patients so that others do not make the same mistakes. Mistakes are simply a reality of the complexity of the healthcare world where knowledge is evolving and never fully complete. The possibility of mistakes must be part of the expectations discussed in the healthcare relationship.

As Seligman points out, 'Without the individual as a wilful actor there can be no trust since there does not exist that peculiar type of risk to which trust is a solution.'[25] Seligman sees risk as framing life's contingencies internally rather than in terms of an external system.[26] Internal framing leaves it to the individual involved to negotiate their own terms of managing the risks and working out in whom trust can be placed. External framing leaves it to the system to protect people from damage. Trust is in the system, rather than the individual. The system is, in reality, a group of people outside the particular patient/healthcare professional relationship. Power is taken from the patient/healthcare professional relationship and placed with an external agent.

Individuals are always part of some system and systems are made up of individuals. Systems are checks on individuals and individuals are checks on systems. Individuals are moulded by systems and they also mould systems. It would be difficult, if not impossible, to demonstrate empirically whether placing trust in a system is more effective than placing trust in an individual. Ideally, both the individual healthcare professional and the healthcare system should be trustworthy. They should complement each other, rather than one being superior to the other. There has been a shift from the internal values of the individual healthcare professional to systems of control and audit within which the healthcare professional works. The individual healthcare professional's main compass and guide used to be the norms and values of their profession. Now, it is more likely to be the norms and values of external codes that change patients into 'consumers',[27] and management targets that allocate appropriate 'outcomes' and 'outputs'.[28]

As Onora O'Neill said in the preface to her BBC Reith Lectures in 2002:

> some fashionable ways of trying to make institutions and professionals trustworthy undermine our abilities to place and refuse trust with discrimination ... We set detailed performance targets for public bodies, but are complacent about the perverse incentives they create. We try to micromanage complex institutions from the centre, and wonder why we get overcomplex and inadequate rather than good and effective governance.[29]

For example, Tallis shows a 25 per cent rise in what he calls 'health quangos' and 'watchdogs' in the United Kingdom between 1997 and 2003.[30]

Before the Cartwright Report's inquiry into cervical cancer research in New Zealand in 1988, the Medical Research Council, under the Medical Research Council Act 1950, developed a procedure for the ethics of experimentation.[31] Applicants to the Medical Research Council for project or programme grants were 'required to sign an ethical agreement stating they had read and agreed to abide by the principles' in the Medical Research Council's brochure *Projects and Programme Grants*.[32] Ethical guidelines for research using human participants, based on the Declaration of Helsinki of 1964, were 'first formally adopted in New Zealand in 1968'.[33] These guidelines were developed by the Medical Research Council and incorporated elements relating to informed consent and vulnerable research participants.[34] However, these guidelines did not cover researchers from non-medical backgrounds. The Medical Research Council and the Department of Health set up the Health Services Research Committee, which produced an ethical *Guide to Health Services Research in New Zealand* in 1983.[35] In May 1984, the Medical Research Council set up the Committee on Ethics in Research.[36]

Thus, before Dr Green embarked on his experiment (see Chapter I), in which he chose not to inform his patients they had symptoms of cervical cancer in the hope that the cancer would be benign, he had an ethical requirement to inform his patients.[37] The problem was not caused by a lack of ethical guidelines. Peer review had broken down and a working party, which was asked to review the particular research proposal, focused on the need to repair broken relationships without dealing with the central question – namely the dispute between doctors about whether the proposal should continue.[38] Whilst healthcare professionals, like other professionals, should display the utmost courtesy to one another and refrain from interfering in one another's work as a matter of etiquette, this does not remove their primary obligation to their patient. If a healthcare professional considered another healthcare professional was putting a patient in jeopardy, then they should intervene.[39] The culture of not questioning a senior healthcare professional's approach was the core problem in Dr Green's case, rather than any lack of ethical guidelines. Without a strong desire to create a trustworthy environment, adding more and more external controls will not necessarily make any difference to the degree of trust between patients and healthcare professionals.

Since the Cartwright Report in New Zealand, we have spawned a raft of ethics committees. All District Health Boards were required to establish ethics committees for the purpose of considering ethical issues. A 2001 Committee of Inquiry report into cervical screening in Gisborne found that there were unacceptable levels of under-reporting of cervical cancer.[40] The report found that the ethics committee had unwittingly contributed to the delay of a comprehensive evaluation of the screening programme.[41] The 2002 review of progress in implementing the recommendations of the Gisborne cervical screening inquiry report found that day-to-day operations were interrupted and affected by ongoing emphasis on external recommendations and expectations.[42] It was found that ongoing sustainability of operations is difficult to achieve when activities and staff are exposed to constant review from external parties.

More ethics committees and more scrutiny do not necessarily create more trust. The committees have their own agendas, one step removed from the healthcare professional/patient relationship. The different layers of systems create their own problems. The management system is concerned primarily with economic efficiency and minimising risk for the 'business'. The disciplinary system is concerned primarily with the imposition of external norms that may or may not inhibit treatment in the particular case. The internal professional system is concerned primarily with the best currently available methods of treatment for the patient's condition. There will inevitably be conflicts between these systems and choices that have to be made by individual healthcare professionals and their patients. The patient has to trust that the healthcare professional will make the best choices for him or her and explain the options in a way that they understand. The systems themselves cannot make choices or set out options, so ultimately the individual healthcare professional has to work out the best option and the patient has to trust that the healthcare professional has chosen the best option. There comes a point in every healthcare decision when all we have is trust.

Regulation itself is dependent on trust – trust in the system rather than trust between the healthcare professional and their patient. Such regulations bring with them their own problems; questions like how can one trust the regulators arise. The regulators and those who apply the regulations may well have agendas of their own. Excessive regulations make it more difficult for trust between healthcare professionals and patients to flourish. Healthcare professionals can spend a great deal of time worrying about regulations, which means they have less time to build a relationship of trust with their patients. Healthcare professionals and patients alike are supposed to put their trust in regulations and systems created by unknown, faceless people who are far removed from the immediate decisions that have to be made.

Tallis uses the example of cardiopulmonary resuscitation (CPR) to show what happens when a healthcare professional's judgment is replaced by regulations.[43] CPR on elderly, fragile patients can sometimes result in broken ribs, brain damage and, at worst, leave the patient in a persistent vegetative state.[44] Some people view these results as worse than death itself. The fear of reprisal by family members if the elderly patient dies may mean that a precautionary attitude is taken and CPR is administered against the instincts and judgment of the medical professional.[45] As Tallis says, 'prudence will be a higher value than compassion'.[46] If the basis for the patient's trust is in the regulations rather than in the healthcare professional, patients become seen as potential complainants rather than patients. The focus shifts from a healthcare professional with the paramount duty to protect and care for the patient, to a healthcare professional who is primarily concerned with protecting him or herself. As Tallis eloquently puts it, 'The Hippocratic precept of good medicine is "First do no harm"; that of defensive medicine is "First cover your ass".'[47]

Nurturing trust

The function of healthcare law should be to provide the space for trust between healthcare professionals and patients to thrive. Trust is a fragile value that can be pulled in different directions. As Baier says, 'Over-willingness to excuse untrustworthiness, like undue distrust, may not merely deprive me of a good but destroy a mini-system, a little network of mutually beneficial expectations.'[48] By way of contrast, 'Demanding one's rights belligerently is certainly one way to destroy trust, but never standing up for them or not bothering to find out if they are being ignored is an equally effective destroyer of a network of trust.'[49] Giving rights out, without their corresponding duties, is a sure-fire way to create a climate of belligerent insistence on rights. A right to informed consent not only places a duty on healthcare professionals to give clear and accurate information, it also places a duty on patients to listen to that information and assess it.

Baier says we can only really measure trust on a case-by-case basis and tentatively puts forth the general thesis that:

> trust is appropriately placed in those who, for whatever motives, welcome the equalization of power, who assist the less powerful and renounce eminence of power, who, when they ask us to delay the accounting of their use of discretionary power, do so for reasons that we will eventually see to have been good (as good parents correctly tell their young children "one day you will understand, but not yet. And it is so that you will one day understand, and be my equal, that I ask you now to trust me").[50]

A welcoming of the equalisation of power is the central idea to Baier's proposal for when trust is most likely to thrive. Actual equalisation of power is difficult to measure and may be impossible to achieve. Using Baier's analysis, the most trustworthy attitude is to strive to equalise power as best as one can, regardless of the circumstances, rather than simply exercising power over another. In the healthcare context, whilst the healthcare professional has the superior medical understanding, they can, by sharing that knowledge with the patient via good communication, demonstrate an attitude of power equalisation. The patient has some power, in their knowledge of their own body and how it feels. By listening to this information, the healthcare professional cultivates the climate of trust that is much more likely to lead to a better diagnosis.

Care, empathy and respect for others are the key qualities necessary for an attitude of equalising power and thereby fostering trust. Care in the sense of doing what is best for the other person, empathy in trying to understand how they feel, and respect in the sense that they are my equal as a human being. David Rogers believes that healthcare professionals should be social activists who 'address social wrongs which interfere with mental and physical well-being as well as more obvious and direct health hazards'.[51] They should become 'the vocal and articulate advocate for the health care of the have-nots in our societies'.[52]

At the heart of trust is the balance between belief that another has goodwill toward me, and the risk that I am vulnerable to their ill will. Ideally, trust thrives in an environment where there is love and care for others. Such environments are not easy to find in the modern world of external measures, performance indicators and the need to demonstrate outputs. These environments start more from the premise of distrust of the individual to make their own decisions. It is ironic that one of the first major controllers of professions was Margaret Thatcher, who believed passionately in Milton Friedman's economic model of the free market.[53] The emphasis was on creating competition and reducing government expenditure.

There is a theory that we need to institutionalise distrust before we can have trust.[54] This theory has a long philosophical history. In *The Republic*, Plato's older brother Glaucon debates with Socrates that human beings are inclined to do bad things in their own self-interest and they need fear of detection and punishment to keep them in line.[55] Machiavelli takes a similar view of human nature in his treatise *The Prince*, where it is recommended that those in power should use their power to keep others in fear of repercussions if they do not act accordingly.[56] Ideas of transparency, accountability, checks and balances have grown from this theory. The reality of the collapse of the economies in the United States and the United Kingdom has shown these ideas are only as good as those applying them. Even worse, they have the potential to lull people into a sense that everything must be all right, rather than encourage them to make their own judgment. General ideas of transparency, accountability and checks and balances are a bit like a used-car salesperson saying, 'This car has been independently tested,' which can mean anything from a genuine, independent test to a light once-over by the salesperson's friend.

Diego Gambetta, drawing together a collection of essays on trust, concludes that:

> Trust . . . is a particular level of the subjective probability with which an agent assesses that another agent or group of agents will perform a particular action, both *before* he can monitor such action (or independently of his capacity ever to be able to monitor it) *and* in a context in which it affects *his own* action . . . [A probability] high enough for us to consider engaging in some form of cooperation with him.[57]

Each individual has to make that choice for him or herself and take that risk. Some will trust because they have dealt with the healthcare professional before; others will trust because of the reputation of the healthcare professional; still others will trust because they believe the healthcare system they are entering is one that can be trusted. Ideally, trust should be based on the care and attitude shown to the patient by the healthcare professional. When the patient is in a coma, there is no opportunity to make a decision about trust. The hope is that you will be given appropriate medical care. If there is too much distrust, either because of previous let-downs or because of a perception of distrust, then the healthcare system would break down. No one would take their loved ones to a hospital or emergency clinic.

Richard Wilkinson and Kate Pickett show in their book *The Spirit Level* that the greater the income inequality in a society, the less trust there is between members of that society.[58] As the authors say, 'Imagine living somewhere where 90 per cent of the population mistrusts one another and what that must mean for the quality of everyday life – the interactions between people at work, on the streets, in shops, in schools,'[59] and I would add, when you go to see the doctor. John Barefoot and others explain that higher levels of trust mean that people feel secure and, in fact, live longer.[60] Greater hierarchal control is likely to create more inequality and more distrust. Those at the top of the hierarchy exercise control on the assumption that, without it, the healthcare professional may not be trusted to do the job. Control is likely to lead to resentment and begrudging compliance, on paper at least, which takes up valuable time. This time could be better spent building a relationship of trust with the patient and cultivating open and honest reflection and dialogue between healthcare professionals. Both measures would enhance the healthcare professional's work.

As Baier is quoted as saying so eloquently at the beginning of this chapter, trust depends on 'goodwill' in the sense of doing what is best for one another.[61] Trust is morally decent and it 'does not rely on successful threats held over the trusted' or on 'successful cover-ups of breaches of trust'.[62] Human nature is infinitely flexible and adaptable. If we expect the worst in people, then it should come as no surprise that we will receive the worst. If we expect the best in human nature, then we may just receive the best. The destiny of sustaining a trusted profession is in the hands of healthcare professionals themselves: no one else can do it for them. Just as individuals become trusted through their actions over time, so too do healthcare professionals.

Simply removing external controls and bureaucracies will not automatically make healthcare professionals more trustworthy. Trust is an earned value. It must be worked for, every day, in every interaction. It must be forged in the soul of every healthcare professional. In order for it to be forged in their souls, healthcare professionals must be toughest on themselves – no one else can do it for them. It either comes from within or it does not come at all. Trust is not so much prescribed but created and fostered by an attitude of mind. At the core of trust is the desire to equalise power, to treat others as we would want to be treated ourselves. This is not always easy for a profession that has so much power and status bestowed on it by society. Tom Bailey, in his article 'On Trust and Philosophy', argues that for trust to flourish in the healthcare world, healthcare professionals must:

> take responsibility for my health . . . If I trust the doctor to prescribe me appropriate treatment, I rely on her because I believe that she has taken responsibility for her role in my decisions about my health. Indeed, I may even allow her to effectively make these decisions for me.[63]

Bailey goes on to say that:

> taking responsibility implies that they cannot intentionally lead us to rely on them in ways they cannot or will not satisfy, since this would conflict with our basic reason for trusting them. They must therefore be at least competent and honest.[64]

Competence and honesty are essential ingredients of trust. Competent healthcare experiences build trust, in that it becomes easier for the patient to believe that the positive experience is likely to happen again. Honesty also builds trust. For example, if something goes wrong, honesty about what happened and how and why it occurred keeps the lines of communication and trust open. Competence and honesty build on one another and encourage healthcare professionals to take responsibility for their actions and to enhance the wellbeing of their patients. Equalising power also provides a strong foundation for trust, by ensuring both parties take an active role in improving the patient's wellbeing.

Even if we accept the contestable assumption that human beings act only out of self-interest, there are self-interest reasons why a system based on trust is better for us all. Without trust, everyone must be watched over. Even then, if we have no trust, we cannot rely on those who do the watching over. We are on our own, yet we cannot always look after our own health. There are times we need to rely on others and be able to trust them to do the right thing.

The choices are relatively simple. If healthcare professionals want to cling to power and status, they will be controlled by external regulators more and trusted by patients less. This in turn means that more patients are likely to suffer the effects of defensive medicine, where things are done to protect healthcare professionals from future consequences, rather than in the best interests of the particular patient. Costs are driven up, when the money could be much better spent on prevention and healthcare for those who really need it.

The first way to equalise power within society is for healthcare professionals to make themselves readily available in emergency situations regardless of the circumstances. Many healthcare professionals have this attribute in abundance and travel to third-world and war-torn countries to help highly vulnerable people who have no power at all. Even in more typical settings, most healthcare professionals feel an inner duty to use their knowledge and skill to help those in emergency need.

The other side of trust is risk. Trust always has an element of risk. When a person's health is at risk in an emergency situation, a healthcare professional takes the risk that they may or may not get the diagnosis right. The fact that they are prepared to take the risk for the good of another means we should take the risk to trust them. From this basis begins the building of a relationship of trust within society.

Notes

1 Baier, A, *Moral Prejudices: Essays on Ethics*, Cambridge: Harvard University Press, 1994, p 99.
2 Ibid.
3 Hume, D, *A Treatise of Human Nature*, Selby-Bigge, L and Nidditch, P (eds), Oxford: Clarendon Press, 1978, p 497.
4 Op. cit., Baier, p 128.

5 Ibid, p 123.
6 Ibid, p 128.
7 Ibid, p 123.
8 Ibid.
9 Ibid, pp 123–124.
10 Ibid, p. 125.
11 Hippocrates, 'Epidemics', in Jones, W (trans.), *Hippocrates Volume I*, Cambridge: Harvard University Press, 1948, p 165.
12 Hardin, R, *Trust and Trustworthiness*, New York: Russell Sage Foundation, 2002, p 3.
13 Ibid, p 1.
14 Cronin, A, *Dr Finlay's Casebook*, London: BBC, 1962.
15 The night before she had been to a private emergency clinic with stomach pains and given medicine for what was perceived to be constipation. The pain became worse during the next day and after seeing her GP the family member was referred to the emergency department of a public hospital for tests.
16 Tallis, R, *Hippocratic Oaths: Medicine and its Discontents*, London: Atlantic Books, 2005, p 76.
17 Ibid.
18 Ibid, p 79.
19 Ibid.
20 McEvoy, V, 'The Incredibles', *Harvard Medical Alumni Bulletin* 79, 2006.
21 Seligman, A, *The Problem of Trust*, Princeton: Princeton University Press, 1997.
22 Ibid, p 174.
23 See, 'DNR', Season 1, Episode 9, *House*, Los Angeles: Fox Broadcasting Company, 2004.
24 Groopman, J, *How Doctors Think*, Melbourne: Scribe Publications, 2007, p 21.
25 Op. cit., Seligman, p 172.
26 Ibid, pp 172–173.
27 See the Code of Health and Disability Services Consumers' Rights as prescribed by the Health and Disability Commissioner (Code of Health and Disability Services Consumers' Rights) Regulations 1996, which refers to all patients as consumers.
28 See generally, Ministry of Health, *Statement of Intent 2010-13*, Wellington: Ministry of Health, 2010, which strategises towards positive 'outcomes' and 'outputs' for the future of healthcare in New Zealand.
29 O'Neill, O, *A Question of Trust: The BBC Reith Lectures 2002*, Cambridge: Cambridge University Press, 2002, pp vii–viii.
30 Op. cit., Tallis, p 104.
31 Ministry of Health, 'History of Health and Disability Ethics in New Zealand' (2007) Health and Disability Ethics Committees http://www.ethicscommittees.health.govt.nz.
32 Ibid.
33 Ibid.
34 Ibid.
35 Ibid.
36 Ibid.
37 Cartwright, S, *The Report of the Cervical Cancer Inquiry 1988*, Auckland: Government Printing Office, 1988.
38 Ibid, p 87.
39 Cartwright, S, 'Ethics and Patient Rights', *The Report of the Cervical Cancer Inquiry 1988*, Auckland: Government Printing Office, 1988, pp 127–176.

40 Duffy, A, Barrett, S and Duggan, A, *Report of the Ministerial Inquiry into the Under-Reporting of Cervical Smear Abnormalities in the Gisborne Region*, Wellington: Committee of Inquiry Report, 2001.
41 Ibid, p 11.
42 McGoogan, E, *Review of Progress to Implement the Recommendations of the Gisborne Cervical Screening Inquiry Report*, Wellington: Office of the Auditor General, 2002, at [11].
43 Op. cit., Tallis, pp 102–108.
44 Ibid, p 106.
45 Ibid. p 105.
46 Ibid.
47 Ibid, p 108.
48 Op. cit., Baier, p 150.
49 Ibid, p 151.
50 Ibid, pp 180–181.
51 Rogers, DE, 'On Trust: A Basic Building Block For Healing Doctor-Patient Interactions', *Journal of the Royal Society of Medicine* 87, 1994, p 5.
52 Ibid.
53 See generally, Frazer, W, 'Milton Friedman and Thatcher's Monetarist Experience', *Journal of Economic Issues* 16, 1982.
54 Sztompka, P, 'Trust in Democracy and Autocracy', in *Trust: A Sociological Theory*, Cambridge: Cambridge University Press, 1999.
55 See, Cornford, F, *The Republic of Plato*, London: Oxford University Press, 1970, p 44.
56 Machiavelli, N, *The Prince*, London: Penguin Books, 2003, pp 48, 52–54.
57 Gambetta, D (ed.), *Trust: Making and Breaking Cooperative Relations*, New York: Blackwell Publishers, 1990, p 217.
58 Wilkinson, R and Pickett, K, *The Spirit Level: Why More Equal Societies Almost Always Do Better*, London: Allen Lane, 2009.
59 Ibid, p 54.
60 Barefoot, J *et al*, 'Trust, Health and Longevity', *Journal of Behavioural Medicine* 21, 1998.
61 Op. cit., Baier, p 99.
62 Ibid, p 123.
63 Bailey, T, 'On Trust and Philosophy' (2002) BBC Reith Lectures: The Philosophy of Trust http://www.open2.net/trust/on_trust/on_trust1.htm. This article is associated with Baroness O'Neill's 2002 Reith Lecture, *A Question of Trust*.
64 Ibid.

Chapter 3

The emergency situation
A premium on trust

Legally classifying the emergency case

In an emergency situation, patients' lives and wellbeing usually depend on immediate medical intervention. However, emergency patients are often unconscious and unable to make medical choices. All they have is trust that the appropriate medical decisions will be made. Such emergency patients are totally dependent on healthcare professionals. There is little or no time to consult written guidelines or ethics committees, or even other members of the profession. Trained instincts take over. The unconscious patient and their family must trust that the right medical interventions will be made. The healthcare professional must trust their training, knowledge and judgment. They have to rely on their internal resources.

In terms of theories of trust, it may appear that there is unequal power in the situation. The patient is powerless, unconscious, limp, perhaps barely alive. The healthcare professional is conscious, with discretion to make choices about what to do, which gives them power. But it is power limited by the pressure of the circumstances, where quick decisions have to be made, often with limited resources. There is no time to think, 'I have unlimited power to do what I like with this patient.' It is much more likely to be, 'I had better get this right otherwise this patient is going to die.' The pressure of the situation is an equaliser of power. Human empathy and compassion, together with professional training and instincts, create the potential for trust.

There are very few examples of psychopathic healthcare professionals who enjoy watching a patient die while they do nothing, or deliberately do the wrong thing. Such criminal behaviour in the emergency situation, or any situation, is an aberration but it is no reason to create a myriad of external codes and audits to cover emergency situations. Internal goodwill, training, dedication and competence are all that the unconscious patient can rely on at the moment of medical intervention. Each one of these moments is dependent on personal medical judgment. The most the unconscious patient can hope for is that the healthcare professional has sufficient knowledge to work out what needs to be done, the judgment to choose the right option and the skill to carry it out. The outcome is utterly dependent on the training, the experience and the state of mind of the healthcare professional. They have to be able to train themselves to do the right thing in the situation, or at the very least, if there is any time to do so, to be able to confer with a colleague about the available options.

The common law recognises the immediacy of the situation. As Lord Donaldson states in the House of Lords:

> In an emergency a doctor has little time to ponder the choices available. He must act in the best interests of his patient, as he sees them, but he can be more readily forgiven if he errs in his judgment.[1]

The common law principle trusts the doctor to do his or her best in the situation and is prepared to forgive and continue that trust if the pressure of the situation leads to an understandable error of judgment.

The Code of Consumers' Rights does not use the word 'forgiveness'.[2] It is predicated on the patient's best interests, which is the same as the common law, but adds the requirement of taking reasonable steps to ascertain the views of the 'consumer' (the new word for patient) or taking account of the views of other suitable persons who are interested in the welfare of the 'consumer' and available to give advice to the provider.[3] There is an out clause that says it is not a breach of the Code of Consumers' Rights if 'reasonable actions' have been taken in the circumstances to give effect to the rights set out in the Code of Consumers' Rights.[4]

The emphasis in the Code of Consumers' Rights is on taking account of the views of the patient, or the views of those close to the patient.[5] The common law emphasis is that in emergency situations a doctor is 'lawfully entitled and probably bound to carry out such treatment as is necessary to safeguard the life and health of that patient'.[6] The common law approaches the problem through the vehicle of necessity – treatment is to be given that is 'necessary to meet the emergency and such as needs to be carried out at once and before the patient is likely to be in a position to make a decision for himself'.[7]

The Canadian courts posit the issue of emergency medical treatment as a conflict between the right of a person to the inviolability of their person, except by consent, and the duty of the healthcare professional to act to save a patient's life. In *Marshall v Curry*,[8] the Canadian courts gave overriding paramountcy to the healthcare professional's duty to act to save a patient's life. The duty of a healthcare professional to save lives gives unconscious patients the right to be treated, which is what we are all likely to want if we are unconscious and not able to consent. Overemphasis on the right of informed consent, which places a duty on doctors to make sure they have fully informed the patient, or in the case of the unconscious patient, informed others close to the patient, may well protect the patient's right to consent. However, in an emergency situation, it distracts attention from the right to be treated and the duty of the healthcare professional to act.

A medical procedure should be carried out on a patient incapable of giving their consent, provided that the procedure is in the patient's best interests.[9] A procedure 'will be in their best interests if, but only if, it is carried out in order either to save their lives, or to ensure improvement or prevent deterioration in their physical or mental health'.[10] Where children are involved, the duty to save the patient's life in the emergency situation over-rides consent or refusal of consent of others such as parents who normally have legal authority to make decisions about their children. In *Gillick v West Norfolk and Wisbech Area Health Authority*,[11] the House of Lords held that a doctor could carry out treatment on a child in an emergency situation, where it is vital for the survival or health of the child, even if a parent opposes it, or where it is impossible to alert a parent before the medical intervention.[12] An analysis of the justifications for acting without consent provides the basis for determining when and how emergency decisions should be made about adults.

Justifications for acting without consent

There are four underlying justifications for allowing medical intervention without consent in emergency situations:

Ordinary conduct of everyday life

One justification is that physical intervention without consent in medical emergencies is acceptable because it is part of the ordinary conduct of everyday life. Unwanted physical contact that is part of everyday life, such as 'jostling experienced by travellers on public transport . . . the touching to obtain atten-tion, the congratulatory slap on the back and the unwelcomely firm hand-shake', is an exception to the general principle that any non-consensual touching is an assault.[13] The rationale for the everyday-life exception is that there is some inevitable physical contact associated with everyday life. For example, brushing past someone in a small corridor or tapping a stranger on the shoulder to ask him or her for the time is seen as part of everyday life. Even though these actions are not consensual, they are not normally viewed as assault. However, the everyday-life exception is not particularly relevant when it comes to emergency medical situations. Emergency situations do not fit into the ordinary conduct of everyday life because, by their very nature, they are much more extreme. The everyday-life exception suggests that if you travel by crowded train, other passengers may well bump into you. Those who wish to avoid this may choose another form of transportation. However, the unconscious patient in an emergency situation has no such choice. Neill LJ rightly said that the ordinary conduct of everyday-life exception should be reserved for 'the commonplace events of daily life and I would not seek to extend it to cover surgical procedures which may include amputations'.[14]

Implied consent

A second justification is that patients have automatically impliedly given their consent to medical intervention in emergency situations. If the patient had been conscious, this is what they would have wanted, therefore it is implied that their consent has been given, even though they are unconscious. This justification is reflected in the Code of Consumers' Rights, which places an emphasis on finding out the patient's views and the views of others. The Code of Consumers' Rights places a duty on the medical profession to find out what the patient might want.[15] As Neill LJ explains, such a justification may suggest that there is 'some duty to look at earlier medical records to discover the patient's attitude when conscious to particular forms of treatment'.[16] This creates uncertainty for the healthcare professional as to how far they should go to treat an unconscious patient.

The dilemma between a patient's choice to refuse treatment and a healthcare professional's desire to save life is best exemplified by the case of a Canadian woman who was a practising Jehovah's Witness.[17] The woman came into the hospital after a serious car crash in an unconscious state and needing a blood transfusion to save her life.[18] The doctor found a card in the woman's purse, which said that, in case of emergency, she did not want a blood transfusion because she was a Jehovah's Witness, and that she understood the implications of this decision.[19] The doctors checked with her siblings who confirmed that, as far as they were aware, their sister was still a practising Jehovah's Witness. The patient's condition began to deteriorate, thus the doctor went ahead and gave her the blood transfusion, despite the fact she was a Jehovah's Witness.[20]

When the patient recovered, she brought an action against the doctor alleging negligence, assault, battery and religious discrimination.[21] The patient's battery claim against her doctor was successful because the doctor had given the patient a blood transfusion against her declared wishes.[22] The patient was awarded damages of $20,000.[23] This decision was ultimately upheld in the Ontario Court of Appeal.[24] The legal analysis in this decision is sound because the patient had previously withdrawn her consent to a blood transfusion, thus for the doctor to perform a blood transfusion on this patient was an act of battery.

Section 11 of the New Zealand Bill of Rights Act 1990 recognises that: 'Everyone has the right to refuse to undergo any medical treatment.'[25] This principle is essentially a restatement of the common law principle of the inviolability of a person's bodily integrity.[26] In the cold light of a courtroom, with the patient whose rights have been infringed sitting there, it is not difficult to see why a Court would uphold their right to refuse medical treatment. It is quite different in the pressure of an emergency, where life-and-death decisions have to be made immediately or it will be too late. If, in the Canadian case, there had been no time to check the patient's handbag or contact her family, then the doctor would not have been acting against the expressed wishes of the patient, because they would not have known about them. The judge would have been likely to acquit them. The patient may also have been able to forgive the doctor, because the doctor would have acted to save their life, with no knowledge that the patient would have wanted anything different. Too heavy a burden on emergency workers to find out what a patient may or may not have wanted is likely to lead to hesitation and loss of life.

Even when it appears obvious what a patient might want, such as in the Canadian case, there can still be lingering doubts. What if the woman had changed her mind that day about practising the Jehovah's Witness faith and had not dispensed with the card? What if the woman had the card but hoped it would not be taken literally and that blood would be given? It is easy to know these things once the person is conscious again and can tell us. What if the woman did not have the card but there was a church notice from the Jehovah's Witness church in her bag and, when the doctors rang up her family, they said she would not want a blood transfusion? What weight should be put on the family's views when it is not known for sure that the patient would refuse the blood? These scenarios create intolerable dilemmas in situations where action must be taken quickly and decisively. A signed, witnessed directive from a patient that they do not want certain treatment in an emergency is a possible exception to the normal principle that a doctor or other healthcare professional should do all they reasonably can to save life. This exception is not without problems. Signed and witnessed directives provide some evidence of what the patient may have wanted at the time they signed the form, and hopefully the witnesses are attesting to the patient's sound mind and the fact that they were not being pressured at the time it was signed. That being said, we are all capable of changing our minds.

The dilemma for the healthcare professional at the life-and-death moment is whether the person who signed the directive still has that belief. A healthcare professional who followed the direction of such a form would be legally protected from any repercussions. Emergency decisions cannot be reached by the application of a code. It will depend on the gravity of the situation, the time available and the resources available as to how far a healthcare professional can go to find out what views the unconscious patient may have. In the end, the healthcare professional has to be able to say to the patient, as if they were conscious – 'I did what I thought you would have wanted me to do.'

Grant Vallance discusses ethical issues surrounding informed consent and the right to refuse treatment in the emergency context.[27] He advocates for a presumption to treat in emergency situations unless the treatment would be a waste of time, or there is 'independent evidence' making it very clear the patient does not want treatment.[28] Vallance, who at the time was a volunteer rural ambulance officer, and his fellow ambulance officer were called urgently to a party where a young man had been stabbed in the arms and abdomen.[29] The wound to the abdomen was potentially life-threatening although his 'vital signs (level of consciousness, pulse, blood pressure, respirations) were good and stable'.[30] The stabbed victim had been drinking and did not want treatment; rather, he wanted to get revenge against his assailant.[31] The police helped the ambulance officers by restraining the victim so that he could be taken to a medical centre for treatment, then transported to the closest hospital and then a bigger 'base hospital' so that he could be properly examined for potentially life-threatening complications.[32] According to Vallance:

> At the time the patient seemed to have a degree of autonomy even though he had been drinking, yet was this sufficient to justify his refusal of treatment? He knew where he was and what had happened and was determined to either go home and "lie down", or go after his assailant.[33]

Yet Vallance was not convinced 'he really understood the potential seriousness of the wound because he did not seem to listen to us or to his friends when we said it could be life-threatening'.[34] Vallance believed that the trauma had affected the patient's competence to make decisions and, taking the patient's refusal at face value, not giving him treatment would not have promoted the patient's overall autonomy. Vallance explained that without treatment the patient would 'probably have died, and considering the circumstances this would not have been the wishes of the patient. He obviously did not want treatment, but also wanted to live'.[35]

Necessity

The third justification is that of necessity. Lord Goff, in *In Re F*,[36] bases necessity on need; the need of the patient to be treated in emergency circumstances where the patient is either temporarily or permanently disabled from consenting. The common law has generally taken a narrow view of necessity. In the famous case of *R v Dudley and Stephens*,[37] four sailors were dying at sea because of lack of food and water. Two of them, Dudley and Stephens, decided to take the life of the cabin boy, Parker, who was the sickest of them and likely to die first.[38] When the case went to court, the court felt that the need of the sailors to save their lives (by eating the dead cabin boy) came second to the principle of the sanctity of the cabin boy's life.[39] There was no necessity for Dudley and Stephens to save their own lives; their highest duty was to sacrifice their lives rather than take the life of the innocent cabin boy.[40] In *R v Dudley and Stephens*,[41] necessity was argued to justify a charge of murder rather than to save a life, so arguably the harm to the individual of acting without their consent is outweighed by the necessity to save their life.

Necessity leaves open the possibility of argument about the degree to which intervention was necessary. Such an analysis takes place after the intervention has happened. Under the justification of necessity, a healthcare professional would be required to ask themselves if it is necessary for them to intervene in this emergency situation. A justification of necessity creates some uncertainty for intervention: how necessary must the circumstances be before justification after the event will be upheld? This justification says 'we trust you to do the right thing if you can show afterwards it was necessary and whether it was necessary or not will be judged by others who were not there at the time'. This is a weak form of trust that has the potential to create doubt and hesitation.

Two cases involving amputations help show where the line is likely to be drawn. In *Jackovach v Yocom*,[42] a 17-year-old boy had jumped from a moving freight train. The boy had landed heavily on his arm after hitting his head on another freight car as he jumped, and was dragged or rolled a distance of between 50 and 80 feet.[43] The medical result was a badly crushed elbow joint and deep laceration to his scalp.[44] At the hospital, the boy was anaesthetised so his head wound could be stitched. While he was under the anaesthetic, it was observed that his arm was too badly damaged to be saved and, if not removed, could ultimately pose 'a menace to the life of the patient'.[45] The doctor chose not to wait for the anaesthetic to wear off in order to obtain the consent of the boy and his parents (whom it had not been possible to contact) to the amputation because of the risk of shock from the second course of anaesthetic necessary to carry out the amputation.[46] An action against the doctor, brought by the boy and his parents, of acting without their informed consent regarding the amputation, was unsuccessful because the court acknowledged that the situation was a life-threatening emergency that required action without consent to preserve the life of the boy.[47]

By comparison, in *Rogers v Sells*,[48] a 14-year-old boy's parents were successful in suing a doctor who amputated their son's right foot, without their consent, after their son had been in a car accident. The physician's evidence was that the boy's right leg was:

> crushed and mangled; that the muscles, blood vessels and nerves were torn and some of the nerves severed, and that the foot had no circulation and that he deemed an immediate amputation necessary under the circumstances in order to preserve the life and health of the boy.[49]

The original jury believed the testimony of a lay witness who said that the leg was not bleeding badly and accepted the patient's evidence that he was still able to wiggle his toes.[50] The jury also believed an expert who said he personally would not have amputated the leg and that there was no real need for haste unless some complications had occurred.[51] There was also time and opportunity to talk with the parents in this case. On appeal, the Supreme Court of Oklahoma was not prepared to overturn this verdict.[52]

Public interest

The strongest justification for medical intervention in emergency cases is that 'it is in the public interest that unconscious patients requiring emergency treatment should be able to receive it and that doctors giving it should not be liable in tort'.[53] This justification says doctors and other healthcare professionals have the expertise to act. We need them to act, we trust them to do the right thing in the situation and it is in all of our interests to place this trust in them because any one of us could be the patient. We do not want them to be worrying about or distracted by legal consequences. We do not want them to practise defensive medicine and avoid emergency situations due to fear of legal consequences if anything goes wrong. Provided the healthcare professional acts in good faith, with the intent to do the best they can in the circumstances, there should be no legal consequences for them. Things will go wrong from time to time. In those situations it is better that the individual who suffered harm be compensated from a public fund. Emergencies, by their very nature, are part of the risk of living in society. They cannot be predicted, they can happen to anyone and we should all combine to contribute to the costs of emergency cases that go wrong. We should forgive healthcare professionals who, acting in good faith, due to the pressure of the situation, sometimes get it wrong. We want to encourage them to act in good faith in similar situations and learn from their experiences.

Those who act in bad faith deliberately to do harm in emergency situations are not fit to be healthcare professionals. Such intentional malice does great harm to trust and must be eliminated. They should face criminal prosecution for their actions and be struck off as a healthcare professional. In New Zealand, a healthcare professional whose actions are a cause of death can only be prosecuted for the criminal offence of manslaughter if their actions or failure to act are a 'major departure from the standard of care expected of a reasonable person to whom that legal duty applies'.[54] This is a legislative indication that, for criminal prosecution to follow in any medical situation, the actions must be well outside normal practice. The provision applies to all medical intervention that causes death. The major departure in the emergency situation would be measured against the normal principles of emergency medicine in the particular situation. The law in this situation really only loses trust when the healthcare professional has gone well outside what would normally be expected.

On 29 August 2005, Hurricane Katrina destroyed the Gulf cities of Biloxi and New Orleans. As a result of the hurricane, levees in New Orleans burst with extensive flooding. This meant that hospitals became isolated. Dr Anna Pou, a head and neck surgeon at Memorial Medical Centre in New Orleans, was on duty when the flooding occurred.[55] She decided to stay in the hospital and ultimately ended up practising medical care outside her normal area of expertise. The shortage of doctors in the crisis meant that Dr Pou took responsibility for the acute-care long-term facility where 'very sick and nearly terminally ill patients' were treated.[56] The extreme conditions caused by the hurricane and the flooding meant resources in the hospital became scarce, thus Dr Pou and other healthcare professionals devised a 'simple priority system for patient evacuation when outside relief finally materialized'.[57] After making many of these difficult medical decisions, Dr Pou was charged with the homicide of four elderly and critically ill patients.[58] Eventually, Dr Pou was exonerated by an Orleans Parish Grand Jury's refusal to indict her.[59] The American Medical Association and the American College of Surgeons supported Dr Pou, emphasising the difficulty of making life-and-death decisions in such extreme circumstances.[60]

After the terrorism events on 11 September 2001 in the United States, and the subsequent anthrax attacks, the US Department of Health and Human Services issued a directive entitled *Bioterrorism and Other Public Health Emergencies – Altered Standards of Care in Mass Casualty Event*.[61] The directive recognises the difficulty of providing healthcare in emergencies with limited resources and recommended that there be immunity from civil or criminal liability under certain circumstances.[62] As Richard Holt said, 'Medical care during such disasters should likely fall under a state's Good Samaritan act to provide freedom from undue legal liability for the providers.'[63]

The consequences of failure to act in emergency circumstances

The English judges in *In Re F*[64] (a case about whether a person with mental incapacity could be sterilised in their own best interests) did not go as far as placing a legal duty on doctors to act. Donaldson J says that doctors are 'probably bound' to act.[65] Butler-Sloss LJ states:

> Once a duty of care of a patient has been assumed by a doctor he may be considered in certain circumstances to have been negligent not to have taken steps to preserve the life or health of his patient including operating where necessary.[66]

Lord Brandon provides an example of patients being received into the casualty department of a hospital, 'which thereby undertakes the care of them'.[67] At this point, 'it will then be the duty of the doctors at that hospital to use their best endeavours to do, by way of either an operation or other treatment, that which is in the best interests of such patients'.[68]

In *Lowns & Anor v Woods & Ors*,[69] the New South Wales Court of Appeal held that a doctor owes a legal duty to attend a person in an emergency who is not the doctor's patient. A mother returned from a walk to find her 11-year-old son, Patrick, who had a history of epilepsy, in the throws of a seizure.[70] The other son was sent to call an ambulance and the daughter to get a doctor. The daughter ran to Dr Lowns' surgery, which was 300 metres from the child's house, to ask him to come and help her brother.[71] The doctor asked the daughter to bring her brother to the surgery. She replied, 'He's having a bad fit, we can't bring him down.'[72] The doctor said to get him an ambulance. She replied, 'We need a doctor. We have already got an ambulance.' The doctor still refused to come to the house.[73] Ambulance officers arrived at the house but could not administer Valium intravenously. Patrick was taken to a medical surgery, but again the efforts to stop the fit were unsuccessful.[74] Eventually, Patrick was taken to a hospital where the fit was abated by very large doses of medication.[75] Throughout the whole sad episode, Patrick was deprived of oxygen to the brain and thereby suffered major brain damage and quadriplegia.[76] Action was brought against Dr Lowns for failing to attend, and Dr Procopis, a paediatric neurologist, who had told the parents that if Patrick had a seizure, he was to be taken to a hospital as quickly as possible. The claim against Dr Procopis was that he had failed to inform the parents about rectal Valium and how to use it in emergencies.[77] The trial judge, Badgery-Parker J, went against the preponderance of expert witnesses who said that Dr Procopis' advice was consistent with the highest standards of medical practice in Australia at the time.[78] Badgery-Parker J preferred to follow the minority opinion of a specialist practising in the United Kingdom, that Dr Procopis had breached his duty of care to the patient.[79]

Section 27(2) of the Medical Practitioners Act 1938 (NSW), which was in force at that time, said that it was professional misconduct for a doctor to fail to attend to a person without reasonable excuse.[80] The majority of the New South Wales Court of Appeal (Kirby P and Cole JA) read this provision, which applies only to disciplinary action and not civil liability, as an indicator that doctors should owe a legal duty to intervene in emergency situations.[81] The fact that Dr Lowns was physically not far away from Patrick, knew what the appropriate treatment was and what might have happened if it was not carried out, and the fact that he was deemed to be competent to carry it out, led to the imposition of the duty of care.[82] It was material to the decision that the doctor was acting as a doctor at the time the emergency arose, and that he was not involved in any other professional activity that would have prevented him from treating Patrick.[83] Dr Lowns gave testimony at the trial that, had the conversation taken place between himself and the daughter (which Dr Lowns denied but in which the court preferred the daughter's evidence), he would have and should have gone to treat Patrick.[84]

Underlying the decision was the public expectation that doctors should attend patients in need of urgent attention, but only when they are in a 'professional' as opposed to a 'social' context. A doctor's training and expertise does not suddenly disappear because they are in a social setting. In that setting they may have less recourse to equipment and drugs, but they would be judged according to the means available to them. One commentator has said the distinction 'reflects unvoiced concerns that such a duty must have limits falling short of a duty of constant vigilance and not impose too onerous a burden on the medical profession'.[85]

Both Dr Lowns and the medical profession support the obligation to intervene in emergencies. Representatives, writing for the Medico-Legal Society, said that:

> The old ethic prevails; in an emergency, a doctor must provide the treatment he thinks appropriate, at a place he thinks offering the best support for recovery, certainly the best at that time. This ethic does not discriminate in favour of persons usually being his patients.[86]

The general principle of the common law, apart from exceptions such as the parent/child relationship, is that there is no duty to rescue another person who may be in peril.[87] This means a person can see another person drowning in the harbour and not be under any legal obligation to rescue them, either by raising the alarm or by throwing out a life buoy. There is no common law requirement to be a Good Samaritan. The common law classifies people as 'rugged' individuals who should look after themselves.[88] Ernest Weinrib shows that the most powerful justification for the common law position is that to impose such a duty would infringe individual liberty.[89] If a duty were to be imposed, it would be based on beneficence that varies according to specific circumstances. Weinrib quotes Immanuel Kant who said that, 'the law cannot specify precisely what and how much one's actions should do toward the obligatory end'.[90] Weinrib argues for a general legal duty to rescue in an emergency situation where there is no inconvenience to the rescuer – 'when a rescue can be accomplished without a significant disruption of his own projects, the rescuer's freedom to realize his own ends is not abridged by the duty to preserve the physical security of another'.[91] Weinrib's legal duty would apply to all citizens. The problem is that it is difficult to specify what degree of inconvenience would negate the duty. Terms like no 'significant disruption of his own projects' and 'no inconvenience to himself' are not consistent. 'No inconvenience' is very wide and would limit the duty severely; no 'significant disruption' is narrower but open to a wide variety of interpretations.

What Weinrib does show is that stopping to help in emergencies is an erosion of individual liberty. The fact that doctors feel they have a duty to intervene shows that they are prepared to equalise power by giving up their liberty. This creates the basis for a trust relationship between healthcare professionals and society. The general position of common law is that legal strangers do not have legal duties to rescue anyone. Doctors and emergency healthcare professionals have been placed in the category of legal strangers in the emergency situation.[92] Where there is no doctor/patient relationship, the doctor or healthcare professional is treated like any other citizen who may or may not choose to help. If they do choose to help, the common law gives more room for forgiveness and potential error, given the pressures of the situation.

Lord Hoffman expresses the rationale for the reluctance of the common law to impose a duty on 'legal strangers' in emergency situations in *Stovin v Wise*.[93] Lord Hoffman explains that imposing a duty on strangers to act may be too heavy a burden because it interferes with the citizen's individual liberty to go about their business, and means that citizens have to give up their resources, time and effort on behalf of the state without any compensation.[94]

The English Court of Appeal in *Kent v Griffiths & Ors*[95] ruled that an unreasonable delay in response by an ambulance service to an emergency call could be the basis for actionable negligence. Andrew Grubb commented that the decision might be perceived as 'diverting precious financial resources from the treatment and care of patients to compensation claims'.[96]

In *Kent v Griffiths & Ors*,[97] Dr Griffiths, who was treating a pregnant patient in her home, made a 999 call for the patient to be taken to hospital because she was having a serious asthma attack.[98] Two further calls were made when the ambulance did not come. The ambulance arrived 40 minutes after the first call.[99] The trial judge ruled this was 14 minutes longer than would be reasonable in the situation.[100] The patient, Mrs Kent, ultimately suffered respiratory arrest and moderate brain damage, which caused epilepsy and a miscarriage.[101] The trial judge, Turner J, ruled that these consequences would have been avoided if the ambulance's arrival had been more timely.[102] The London Ambulance Service was ordered to pay damages to the patient for the harm caused to her, which could have been avoided if the ambulance arrived more quickly.[103] The English Court of Appeal upheld the trial judge's ruling.[104]

The London Ambulance Service appealed the decision to the Court of Appeal and argued that their failure to respond was before Mrs Kent had been accepted by the ambulance, and thus there was insufficient proximity between Mrs Kent and the London Ambulance Service.[105] The Court of Appeal, led by Lord Woolf MR, rejected this argument, holding the ambulance service's duty began once the first 999 call came in, and distinguished the long line of common law authority that held that there is no duty to be a 'Good Samaritan'.[106] A crucial fact was that there was an available ambulance that had been allocated to this particular emergency. This narrows the scope of the duty to situations where the ambulance service accepts the call and does have the resources available to respond to the emergency. If there were no ambulances available, because they were all out attending to other emergencies, then the issue would have been as to the allocation of resources, which the courts generally do not feel they are suited to adjudicate on.[107] Lord Woolf described the facts as 'unusual in the extreme'.[108] The London Ambulance Service offered no explanation for their unreasonable delay. The times in the ambulance logbook were falsified, and the court was given no explanation as to how and why the lengthy delay occurred.[109]

The crucial facts in *Kent v Griffiths & Ors* were that a named caller gave a specific request about a particular person, which was accepted by the ambulance service. There was an undertaking to help in the circumstances that had not been followed through on.

Lord Woolf attempted to make a distinction between ambulance services and other emergency services such as police, coast guard and fire services by saying that the ambulance service is in a relationship with a patient, like a doctor or nurse, whereas the others are not, their duty being classified as owed to the public at large.[110] However, this argument is not convincing. As Turner J stated in the earlier decision, the underlying rationale for the decision was the public expectation and moral belief that it was:

> offensive to, and inconsistent with, concepts of common humanity if in circumstances such as the present where there had been an unreasonable and unexplained delay in providing the service which LAS were in a position to meet, and had accepted that it would supply an ambulance, the law could not in its turn provide a remedy to the person whose condition was significantly exacerbated in consequence.[111]

The same argument could be applied to police, coast guard and fire services that failed to respond in a timely fashion to an emergency call.

Kevin Williams has provided an analysis of the consequences of the decision in *Kent v Griffiths & Ors*.[112] Over the 10-year period following the decision, 263 claims against the English Ambulance Trust were identified.[113] Thirty-six claims involved delays and 16 claims alleged delay, alongside other concerns such as inadequate treatment.[114] By far the greatest number, 202 claims, were about 'other failures, such as faulty diagnosis, inappropriate medication or equipment failure'.[115] (The remaining nine claims were unclassified because of inadequate case information.) While 48.7 per cent of the claimants received nothing,[116] only 28.3 per cent achieved a settlement resulting in a payment of damages.[117] Of these successful claimants, 69.2 per cent received less than £10,000 in damages, and 25 per cent of the successful claimants received payments above £10,000 but less than £100,000.[118] The highest single payment was £900,000, while the lowest was £500.[119] The average payment came to £38,621.[120] Defence costs paid by the English Ambulance Trust averaged £12,104 per successful claim.[121] Of the delay claims, 80.5 per cent of cases failed, while 67.6 per cent of the other claims failed.[122]

The biggest hurdle to claims was proof of causation – proving, on the balance of probability, that the delay of action at the scene had made their position worse, or lessened their chance of a better outcome. In *Kent v Griffiths & Ors*, Turner J said that 'in meeting a situation of emergency the consequent duty will not be set at an unrealistically or unattainably high level. But that goes to breach, not duty'.[123] Lord Woolf MR used the example of a multiple casualty incident where a quick decision about who should be taken to hospital first is made wrongly. In this situation, liability would not be imposed.[124] Lord Woolf MR put forward causation as the necessary protection against liability for ambulance services, unless their behaviour is exceptionally poor.[125]

Causation is a notoriously difficult legal concept, which can be used either to deflect or impose liability. When the behaviour is 'exceptionally poor', it is more likely that a finding making a causal connection between the behaviour and the harm suffered will be made. When the behaviour is forgivable and understandable in the circumstances, the causal connection will not be made.

Basing the emergency situation on trust

If healthcare law was based on a principle of trust, then the emergency situation would be conceptualised as follows: society trusts healthcare professionals to intervene in emergency situations and use the appropriate skills and judgment for the patient. This trust is based on the fact that healthcare professionals have specialist knowledge and skills that give the patient the best chance of a favourable outcome.

Where a healthcare professional has the opportunity to intervene in an emergency situation but fails to do so, this would be a breach of the trust that has been placed in him or her by society. In a society based on trust, we trust those with the ability or the means to do the right thing for those who are unconscious or otherwise vulnerable and not able to look after themselves. Being trusted to act is a more powerful incentive than being under a legal duty to act.

The driving force for anyone in the healthcare profession should be to contribute to their society and to use their skills, knowledge and training to improve the health of individuals in their society. If healthcare professionals thought for one moment that they only have responsibilities to their patients, then the trust that society places in them would quickly be undermined. Why would we trust someone who has the knowledge and skills to save someone's life but who refuses to do so because that person is not their patient? Such healthcare professionals should face strong sanctions from their profession because any such breach of trust weakens the trust that society has in healthcare professionals.

The New Zealand Medical Disciplinary Tribunal made a finding of 'conduct unbecoming in a medical practitioner' against a doctor who refused to attend one of his regular patients who was giving birth in a nearby house in the early hours of the morning.[126] The reason given by the doctor was that he was not on duty at the time and that an ambulance or on-duty doctor should be called.[127] The Medical Disciplinary Tribunal said the doctor's response 'was less than ideal but understandable in the circumstances he thought existed'.[128] However, ultimately the Medical Disciplinary Tribunal held that Dr de la Porte's conduct was unbecoming of a professional person.[129] This decision quotes an earlier Medical Disciplinary Tribunal decision, which states that a doctor:

> must attend in an emergency whether or not it is a patient of his practice. If he decides not to attend on the basis of what is told to him about the patient's condition and does not call to make his own assessment, he must accept full responsibility in the same way as if he had seen [the patient] in person.[130]

Society has an interest in maintaining the trust that healthcare professionals will do their best to preserve health and wellbeing in emergencies. Once it is undermined, we are all much more vulnerable in the emergency situation.

We may not want to call a doctor in case they do not want to come. Any action should primarily be about restoring trust and preventing further breaches in the future. This may mean that some sanctions are imposed and the individual doctor has to work hard to rebuild the trust that has been damaged by his breach. If the motivation is solely punishment or solely compensating the victim, we miss the most crucial objective, which is to rebuild the trust that has been broken.

A focus on trust as the core principle in the emergency situation helps our understanding of what is likely to amount to a breach of trust. If doctors know they are trusted to intervene and make the appropriate medical decisions in emergency cases, they will first ensure that their training and expertise is up to date so that they are prepared. They must be able to trust their own judgment to do the right thing.

Many of us have been on a plane when a call has gone out for a doctor to help with a sick person. The person may have had a heart attack or stroke, or simply be suffering from food poisoning. The doctor may have just had their meal on the plane, washed down by a glass or two of wine. They may want to just pull the rug over their head and go to sleep. They may be very tired, this being the second leg of a long-haul flight from London to New Zealand. Yet everyone on the flight trusts them to go to the sick person and take the right decisions to make the patient more comfortable, and perhaps even save the patient's life.

A doctor who said, 'I am too tired and I have just had a couple of glasses of wine' and then refused to do anything would not only lose the trust and respect of all those on the plane, but would also weaken the trust in doctors of all those who heard about the situation. However, the doctor who gets up out of their seat and reaches deeply into the recesses of their medical expertise and who uses their best professional judgment in the circumstances fuels our trust in their profession. Such situations equalise power between the medical profession and society. The medical professional is not calling the shots, things are not done at their convenience, so they have to adapt to the situation as best they can. We would be prompt to forgive if everything were not done perfectly. What is crucial is the attitude and drive to do all that can be done in the situation to make the patient better.

Should there be a legal duty to act in an emergency?

There are two choices for how the law could respond in the emergency situation. One is to place a legal duty on doctors to act and do what is necessary in the situation. The confines of the duty would need refinement and some limitations; otherwise it could have the effect of becoming a form of strict liability. Situations could arise where, for example, the doctor may be attending to another patient, and consideration would have to be given as to whether or not the duty to the patient overrides the duty in the emergency situation.

There would also be situations where the doctor may not be in a fit state to act in the situation. For example, the doctor may be in a state of shock themselves and unable to exercise the required judgment. Once a legal duty is created, it is subject to litigation and the pressures and expectations that that creates. The New South Wales Court of Appeal in *Lowns & Anor v Woods & Ors* chose to limit the duty to a professional setting, as opposed to a social setting, when the doctor is not in working mode.[131] The legal duty of the medical professional to intervene in emergency situations would give a corresponding legal right for that intervention to occur and for the treatment to be appropriate in the circumstances.

John Smillie has argued convincingly that tort liability for negligence is difficult to justify on a moral basis, and that its core social functions of compensation and deterrence are performed more fairly and more efficiently by other legal means.[132] Aristotle's theory of corrective justice is cited by Smillie as the justification for the tort of negligence – 'to correct private injustices by transferring wrongful losses from victims to the wrongdoers who caused them'.[133] One act of negligence can cause a massive loss out of all proportion to the act itself. In both of the cases analysed in this chapter – the doctor who failed to respond to Patrick's emergency and in the ambulance case – the loss of life is out of proportion to the failure to act. Loss of life is immeasurable in terms of the harm and distress that it causes. These failures to act were poor professional behaviour, but it would be impossible to fully compensate for the damage that occurred.

In New Zealand, the right to sue for personal injury in the courts (whether through negligence or through any other tort) was removed in 1974. It was replaced by an accident compensation scheme whereby accidents were compensated for out of a public fund. The fear that removing the deterrence of being sued for careless behaviour would increase such behaviour has not been borne out. Two studies show that increased accident-producing behaviour has not occurred. Craig Brown cites a study of motor vehicle accident rates just before and after the removal of the right to sue for personal injury in 1974, which shows that the 'predominantly downward trend in the number of accidents, deaths and injuries that had started prior to 1974 continued and even accelerated after New Zealand adopted the Accident Compensation Act'.[134]

Marie Bismark, and the former New Zealand Health and Disability Commissioner Ron Paterson, show that patient safety has not been adversely compromised by the Accident Compensation Act 2001.[135] As Bismark and Paterson state:

> After thirty years of the ACC and nine years of independent complaint resolution, New Zealand hospitals appear no safer (or more dangerous) than those in other Western countries. The adverse-event rate of 12.9 percent stands midway between the levels recorded in two countries with shared medical traditions in training and practice: Australia (16.6 percent) and the United Kingdom (10.8 percent).[136]

The statistics speak for themselves of the futility of using the courts to compensate for injury and to correct behaviour. The Pearson Royal Commission in England has calculated that about 6.5 per cent of accident victims recover damages.[137] Similar findings were made in Australia, where 'only a very small proportion of disabled people recover compensation under personal injury law'.[138] Yet the Woodhouse Royal Commission in New Zealand worked out that administrative costs such as legal fees, insurance costs, judges' costs and court structure costs account for more than 40 per cent of the amount paid out of the tort system.[139] The 1978 Report of the Royal Commission on Civil Liability and Compensation for Personal Injury (UK) estimated that administrative costs were 45 per cent of the total amount paid out of the tort system.[140] Don Dewees, David Duff and Michael Trebilcock, after analysing the tort system across five categories of accidents, found that, 'The tort system performs so poorly in compensating most victims of personal injury that we should abandon tort as a means of pursuing this compensation objective, turning instead to other instruments.'[141] They also conclude that the court 'tort system performs unevenly in deterring the causes of personal injuries, so its scope should be restricted to situations where its effect seems likely to justify its high cost'.[142]

Court action may be good for lawyers but it is of limited benefit to those who deserve compensation because something went wrong in an emergency situation, either because the treatment itself exacerbated the injury or because there was a failure to act quickly enough, or to act at all, in circumstances where there was opportunity to provide medical services that would have helped.

In any society, there is always the risk of an emergency situation arising, whether from an internal risk, such as a sudden heart attack or asthma attack, or an external risk, such as a car accident or a house fire. The fairest way to compensate for medical and other contingencies that may arise, such as the wrong decision being made under pressure, is for all of us to contribute (according to our means through our taxes) to a public fund that covers this compensation. Smillie would prefer governments 'to provide a fair base level of income support for all disabled people, regardless of cause, leaving those who require more protection to purchase additional cover on the private insurance market'.[143] In *The Damages Lottery*, Patrick Atiyah argues that the role of providing compensation for those injured and harmed in accidents is best left to the personal insurance market.[144] However, Atiyah does note that 'some state social security safety net will still be needed for those who are not otherwise covered at all'.[145]

In *The Spirit Level: Why More Equal Societies Almost Always Do Better*, Richard Wilkinson and Kate Pickett illustrate that perceived trust is lowest in countries that have the greatest income inequality.[146] Wilkinson and Pickett provide a graph that compares 23 countries in relation to data on income inequality and perceptions of trust.[147] These graphs show that the percentage of people who agree that 'most people can be trusted' is less in countries with the highest income inequality.[148] As Wilkinson and Pickett state, 'With greater inequality, people are less caring of one another, there is less mutuality in relationships, people have to fend for themselves and get what they can – so, inevitably, there is less trust.'[149] On the converse, the Scandinavian countries of Sweden, Norway, Finland and Denmark have the highest levels of trust and among the lowest levels of income inequality.

Leaving compensation totally to the market forces of private insurance companies would only work in societies where everyone in that society has the income to afford such insurance. The better option for creating an equality of opportunity to receive compensation is for a state fund to be built up to meet this need.

Because the Accident Compensation Corporation (ACC) Scheme in New Zealand is limited to accidents, those who divulge a long-term condition are not covered. This can lead to arbitrary classification. A past president of the New Zealand Orthopaedic Association, Dr John Matheson, who works in both the public and private sectors, made public comment that the ACC was taking a harder line on how knee and shoulder injuries were considered.[150] Because of the arbitrary distinction in the ACC scheme between accidents (which are covered by the scheme) and long-term medical conditions (which are not), the ACC was rejecting claims on the basis that they were because of degeneration rather than an accident.[151] Dr Matheson said that many of the claims rejected were based on a demonstrable accident.[152] These cases were often successfully reviewed or appealed, but the review and appeal costs are now likely to defeat the cost saving of taking a narrow interpretation of what an accident was. The solution is to provide care or basic cover, as John Smillie proposes, to all who are injured and disabled, no matter what the cause.

The second option is closer to what the present state of common law is. The duty to intervene is not a legal one but an ethical one, based on the doctor's Hippocratic oath to 'first do no harm'. In an emergency situation, the doctor can prevent further harm to the patient. A failure to carry out an ethical duty, in situations where it would be expected, can lead to disciplinary proceedings of professional misconduct, where the actions are generally judged against those of peers.

In England, general medical practitioners are required to provide 'immediately necessary treatment' to 'any person . . . owing to an accident or emergency at any place in its practice area'.[153] The National Health Service (General Medical Services Contracts) Regulations 2004 (UK) classifies a person requiring immediately necessary treatment in an emergency situation as a 'patient'.[154] There is an entitlement for doctors to be paid for such services by their local primary care trust. The regulation is limited to general medical practitioners and their practice area.[155] There is no remedy for anyone whom a general medical practitioner failed to treat, but there is the possibility of disciplinary action against the general medical practitioner. The establishment of such an ethos requires an environment where everyone expects and cares that others in their group are acting for the common good.

Two economists, Ernst Fehr and Simon Gächter, carried out so-called 'public good' experiments, which involved the use of tokens.[156] Groups of four people were given 20 tokens, which they could either contribute to the public pool or keep for themselves over 10 rounds.[157] Investment of one token by a player means that they earn 0.4 tokens (and also lose the initial invested token), but the other players also receive 0.4 by that investment.[158] In essence, investment of one token leads to the group receiving 1.6 tokens.[159] If everyone invests all their tokens, they would all walk away with 32 tokens. If everyone keeps their money and no one invests, they end up with only having their initial 20 tokens each. A 'free-rider' that watches the others invest all their tokens will get the benefit of their investment and still keep his or her 20 tokens. However, if everyone does this, there would be no increase in the original pool. The game is played anonymously so players do not know who is putting money in and who is not.[160] Fehr and Gächter found that this experiment, when played throughout the developed world, led to predictable results. At first, most people do not act selfishly. On average, most contribute half their tokens to the public pool. When there is evidence of free-riding by others, the contribution rates drop. In the end, 70 to 80 per cent of the players free-ride with a much poorer result for the group as a whole.

People fell into three categories, according to Fehr and Gächter. Twenty-five per cent are natural free-riders who put their own interests first. A small minority of participants contribute heavily to the public pot from the beginning and continue to do so even when they see what the free-riders are doing. The largest group begin as contributors to the public pot but when they see what the free-riders are doing, they stop contributing to the public pot.

The economists then changed the rules of the game. Anonymity was removed. At the end of each round everyone knew who the free-riders were. Those who did contribute were given the option of paying in one-third of one of their tokens to punish the free-riders by taking away a whole token of theirs. The result was that free-riders, not surprisingly, began contributing. The vast majority of people want to be responsible and to co-operate for the good of others. They are most likely to continue to do this when they trust others will do the same, which is most likely to happen when others behave transparently and when there is some sanction for those who do not contribute.

As James Surowicki says in his book *The Wisdom of Crowds*, 'the measure of success of laws and contracts is how rarely they are invoked'.[161] Legal actions against medical personnel in emergency situations are not common. This may be because trust is at a premium in such situations. It may be because, as the common law says, we are more forgiving in such situations and less likely to want to punish someone who has tried to do their best in an emergency.

It is in the interests of both the healthcare profession (in order to maintain the trust society places in them) and society for healthcare professionals to try to do the best they can with the facilities available to them in emergency cases.

Expertise is best established by all healthcare professionals voluntarily keeping themselves up to speed, with both the skills and knowledge needed in an emergency situation. In such a situation, healthcare professionals are not necessarily dealing with a patient with whom they have an ongoing relationship. They are dealing with a random member of society, but in another sense they are dealing with society as a whole. Do they want there to be an ongoing relationship of mutual trust with their society or not? If they do, then they will do everything in their power and knowledge to help the wellbeing of the individual in strife. If it does not work out for the best, due to limited resources or the circumstances, then forgiveness is the appropriate response.

If healthcare professionals choose to walk away from the emergency situation and not use their expertise, then in a sense they are undermining the pool of goodwill that has been established by the many other healthcare professionals who have taken immediate action. They are a free-rider in the pool of goodwill and trust toward the healthcare profession. Too many of these free-riders will cause the pool of trust and goodwill will dry up. They must be identified and punished, as were the free-riders in the token game. Those who should have the strongest incentive to expose and expunge such behaviour are the healthcare professionals themselves. It is strongly in their interest to do so, so that the pool of trust is replenished. Leaving complainants to appeal to external bodies such as a Health Commissioner about the lack of intervention is to be complicit with the free-rider and to place a double burden on the person who has already suffered and now suffers again: firstly, because of the failure to intervene, and secondly, the lack of care of the profession to do anything about it.

The paedophilia scandals in the Catholic Church are a classic example of how trust can be undermined – not so much by the criminal acts of the priests and brothers who sexually violated children, which is horrendous in itself, but by the failure of the Church to accept full responsibility for these actions the moment they were aware of them, deal with the perpetrators, apologise to the victims and do all that was necessary to support them.[162] Instead, the perpetrators were not dealt with, simply moved to another parish, and the cries of the victims were ignored. This is the grossest breach of trust – carried out by an organisation that preaches a gospel of love. There was no attempt by the Catholic Church to equalise its immense power with the defenceless victims.

Although a failure to act in an emergency is not in the same category as deliberately sexually violating a child, what these two very different things have in common is a serious abuse of trust. If healthcare professionals want maximum trust from their society, they must be prepared to act in emergencies, even when it is not their patient or it is inconvenient for them. Those healthcare professionals who choose to put their own convenience before the common good undermine that trust. If the healthcare profession as a whole choose to allow that, then they conspire to undermine that trust and have no one to blame but themselves. To act in an emergency situation is to welcome the equalisation of power by assisting a vulnerable human being.

The *World Medical Association Statement on Medical Ethics in the Event of Disasters (Statement on Medical Ethics)*, adopted by the 46th World Medical Association General Assembly in Sweden in September 1994, emphasises the principle of equality. The *Statement on Medical Ethics* says that in 'selecting the patients who may be saved, the physician should consider only their medical status, and should exclude any other consideration based on non-medical criteria'.[163] As the *Statement on Medical Ethics* says, disaster situations are 'characterized by an acute and unforseen imbalance between the capacity and resources of the medical profession and the needs of survivors who are injured whose health is threatened, over a given period of time'.[164]

The pressures of the disaster situation are recognised by the *Statement on Medical Ethics* where it is conceded that 'there may not be enough time for informed consent to be a realistic possibility'.[165] The overriding imperative is to act according to the needs of patients and the resources available. Priorities for treatment in a disaster are to be set 'that will save the greatest number of lives and restrict morbidity to a minimum'.[166] That should be the guiding principle for healthcare generally, not just in disaster situations. Disaster situations focus the mind on what is really important. They can bring out the best in the healthcare profession. Power is equalised by the focus on medical needs and responsibility is taken to save the greatest number of lives and keep morbidity to a minimum. Acting this way in disaster situations provides evidence of a profession that is capable of being trusted.

Notes

1 *In Re F (Mental Patient: Sterilisation)* [1990] 2 AC 1 (HL), p 17.
2 Code of Health and Disability Services Consumers' Rights as prescribed by the Health and Disability Commissioner (Code of Health and Disability Services Consumers' Rights) Regulations 1996.
3 Right 7 of the Code of Health and Disability Services Consumers' Rights.
4 Clause 3 of the Code of Health and Disability Services Consumers' Rights.
5 Right 7 of the Code of Health and Disability Services Consumers' Rights.
6 Op. cit., *In Re F*, p 13.
7 Ibid, p 30.
8 *Marshall v Curry* [1933] 3 DLR 260, p 275.
9 Op. cit., *In Re F*, p 55.
10 Ibid.
11 *Gillick v West Norfolk and Wisbech Area Health Authority* [1986] 1 AC 112 (HL).
12 Ibid, pp 200–201.
13 Op. cit., *In Re F*, p 14.
14 Ibid, p 30.
15 Right 7(4) of the Code of Health and Disability Services Consumers' Rights.
16 Op. cit., *In Re F*, p 30.
17 *Malette v Shulman* [1990] 72 OR (2d) 417.
18 Ibid, pp 418–419.

19 Ibid, p 419.
20 Ibid, p 420.
21 Ibid, p 421.
22 Ibid.
23 Ibid.
24 Ibid, pp 433–435.
25 New Zealand Bill of Rights Act 1990, s 11.
26 A person's right to bodily integrity is not always an absolute right; rather, it depends on the competence of the person. For example, a psychiatric patient ruled to be incompetent may not have the right to refuse treatment. See generally, the Mental Health (Compulsory Assessment and Treatment) Act 1992.
27 Vallance, G, 'Ethical Issues in Obtaining Informed Consent and the Right to Refuse Treatment in the Emergency Context', *Otago Bioethics Review* 1996.
28 Ibid, p 14.
29 Ibid, p 12.
30 Ibid.
31 Ibid.
32 Ibid.
33 Ibid, p 13.
34 Ibid.
35 Ibid.
36 Op. cit., *In Re F*, pp 71–83.
37 *R v Dudley and Stephens* [1884] 14 QBD 273.
38 Ibid, pp 274–275.
39 Ibid, p 287.
40 Ibid.
41 Op. cit., *R v Dudley and Stephens*.
42 *Jackovach v Yocom* 237 NW 444 (Iowa 1931).
43 Ibid, p 445.
44 Ibid, p 446.
45 Ibid, p 449.
46 Ibid.
47 Ibid, pp 449–450.
48 *Rogers v Sells* [1936] 61 P 2d 1018 (Okla 103).
49 Ibid, p 1018.
50 Ibid, pp 1019–1020.
51 Ibid, p 1019.
52 Ibid, p 1020.
53 Op. cit., *In Re F*, p 37.
54 See, Crimes Act 1961, s 150A, which states:

150 A standard of care required of persons under legal duties

(1) This section applies in respect of the legal duties specified in any of sections 151, 152, 153, 155, 156 and 157.

(2) For the purposes of this Part, a person is criminally responsible for—

(a) omitting to discharge or perform a legal duty to which this section applies; or

(b) neglecting a legal duty to which this section applies—

only if, in the circumstances of the particular case, the omission or neglect is a major departure from the standard of care expected of a reasonable person to whom that legal duty applies in those circumstances.

See also, Crimes Act 1961, s 155 which states:

155 Duty of persons doing dangerous acts

Everyone who undertakes (except in case of necessity) to administer surgical or medical treatment, or to do any other lawful act the doing of which is or may be dangerous to life, is under a legal duty to have and to use reasonable knowledge, skill, and care in doing any such act, and is criminally responsible for the consequences of omitting without lawful excuse to discharge that duty.

According to *Adams on Criminal Law*, 'The principal purpose and effect of the "major departure" test in s 150A(2) is to require a high degree of negligence if a person is to be criminally responsible under s 160(2)(b) for manslaughter by negligent omission to perform or observe any of the legal duties specified in s 150A(1).' Robertson, B, *Adams on Criminal Law Student Edition* Wellington: Brookers, 2009, p 283.

55 Holt, R, 'Making Difficult Ethical Decisions in Patient Care During Natural Disasters and Other Mass Casualty Events', *Otolaryngology – Head and Neck Surgery*, 2008;139(2):181–186.
56 Ibid, p 181.
57 Ibid, pp 181–182.
58 Ibid, p 182.
59 Ibid.
60 Ibid.
61 Health Systems Research Inc, *Bioterrorism and Other Public Health Emergencies – Altered Standards of Care in Mass Casualty Events*, Rockville: Agency for Healthcare Research and Quality, 2005.
62 Ibid, p 24.
63 Op. cit., Holt, p 182.
64 Op. cit., *In Re F*.
65 Op. cit., *In Re F*, p 13.
66 Ibid, p 37.
67 Ibid, p 56.
68 Ibid.
69 *Lowns & Anor v Woods & Ors* (1996) Australian Torts Reports 81-376 (NSWCA).
70 Ibid.
71 Ibid.
72 Ibid.
73 Ibid.
74 Ibid.
75 Ibid.
76 Ibid.
77 Ibid.
78 *Woods & Ors v Lowns & Anor* [1995] 36 NSWLR 344.
79 Ibid.
80 The Medical Practitioners Act 1992 (NSW) replaced the 1938 Act with section 31 of the new Act, a close replica of section 27(2) of the old Act.
81 Op. cit., *Lowns & Anor v Woods & Ors*.
82 Ibid.
83 Ibid.
84 Ibid.
85 Day, K, 'Medical Negligence – The Duty to Attend Emergencies and the Standard of Care: *Lowns & Anor v Woods & Ors*', *Sydney Law Review* 18, 1996, p 393.

86 Bain, J and Foster, M, 'Should the Doctor Come?', *Proceedings of the Medico-Legal Society* 6, 1976–80, p 185.
87 Op. cit., *Lowns & Anor v Woods & Ors.*
88 McInnes, M, 'The Question of a Duty to Rescue in Canadian Tort Law: An Answer from France', *Dalhousie Law Journal* 13, 1990, p 112.
89 Weinrib, E, 'The Case for a Duty of Rescue', *The Yale Law Journal* 90, 1980.
90 Ibid, p 267.
91 Ibid, p 292.
92 See generally, *Capital & Counties Plc v Hampshire County Council* [1997] EWCA Civ 3091, [1997] 3 WLR 331, which discussed whether fire authorities were liable in negligence; *Alexandrou v Oxford* [1990] EWCA Civ 19, which discussed whether police officers were liable in negligence; and *OLL Ltd v Secretary of State for Transport* [1997] 3 All ER 897, which discussed whether the coastguard was liable in negligence.
93 *Stovin v Wise* [1996] UKHL 15, [1996] AC 923.
94 Ibid.
95 *Kent v Griffiths & Ors* [2000] EWCA Civ 25, [2000] 2 WLR 1158.
96 Grubb, A, 'Medical Negligence: Liability of Ambulance Service', *Medical Law Review* 8, 2000, p 350.
97 Op. cit., *Kent v Griffiths & Ors* [2000].
98 Ibid, p 1160.
99 Ibid, p 1161.
100 Ibid.
101 *Kent v Griffiths & Ors* [1999] Lloyd's Rep Med 424, p 456. This earlier decision of Turner J's directly precedes the Court of Appeal decision, and generally provides more detailed factual information.
102 Ibid, p 453.
103 Ibid, p 456.
104 Op. cit., *Kent v Griffiths & Ors* [2000], p 1172.
105 Ibid, p 1162.
106 Ibid, p 1164.
107 See generally, Oppenheim, R, 'Resource Allocation and Clinical Negligence Claims', *Clinical Risk* 10, 2004, pp 69–73; and Palmer, E, 'Resource Allocation, Welfare Rights – Mapping the Boundaries of Judicial Control in Public Administrative Law', *Oxford Journal of Legal Studies* 20, 2000, pp 63–88.
108 Op. cit., *Kent v Griffiths & Ors* [2000], p 1172.
109 Op. cit., *Kent v Griffiths & Ors* [1999], pp 446–447.
110 Op. cit., *Kent v Griffiths & Ors* [2000], p 1171.
111 Op. cit., *Kent v Griffiths & Ors* [1999], p 453, which Lord Woolf agreed with and cited in *Kent v Griffiths & Ors* [2000] op. cit., p 1161. This was the same justification that Lord Atkin used in *Donoghue v Stevenson* [1931] UKHL 3, [1932] AC 562.
112 Williams, K, 'Litigation Against English NHS Ambulance Services and the Rule in *Kent v Griffiths*', *Medical Law Review* 15, 2007.
113 Ibid, p 162.
114 Ibid, p 164.
115 Ibid.
116 Ibid, p 168.
117 Ibid, p 169.
118 Ibid.
119 Ibid.
120 Ibid.
121 Ibid.
122 Ibid.

123 Op. cit., *Kent v Griffiths & Ors* [1999], p 453.
124 Op. cit., *Kent v Griffiths & Ors* [2000], p 1171.
125 Ibid.
126 Medical Practitioners Disciplinary Tribunal, *In the Matter of Jacobus Petrus de la Porte*, Decision 70/98/38C, 24 March 1999, at [7.1].
127 Ibid, at [2.5].
128 Ibid, at [5.2.1].
129 Ibid, at [7.1].
130 Ibid, at [6.12].
131 Op. cit., *Lowns & Anor v Woods & Ors*.
132 See generally, Smillie, J, 'The Future of Negligence', *Tort Law Journal* 15, 2007.
133 Ibid, p 3.
134 Brown, C, 'Deterrence in Tort and No Fault: The New Zealand Experience', *California Law Review* 73, 1985, p 1002.
135 Bismark, M and Paterson, R, 'No-Fault Compensation in New Zealand: Harmonizing Injury Compensation, Provider Accountability, and Patient Safety', *Health Affairs* 25, 2006, pp 278–282.
136 Ibid, p 282.
137 Pearson, C, *Report of the Royal Commission on Civil Liability and Compensation for Personal Injury*, London: Her Majesty's Stationery Office, 1978, p 23.
138 Ipp, D, *Review of the Law of Negligence*, Canberra: Commonwealth of Australia, 2002, p 182.
139 Woodhouse, O, *Compensation for Personal Injury in New Zealand: Report of the Royal Commission of Inquiry*, Wellington: Government Printer, 1967, p 25.
140 Op. cit., Pearson, p 26.
141 Dewees, D, Duff, D and Trebilcock, M, *Exploring the Domain of Accident Law: Taking the Facts Seriously*, New York: Oxford University Press, 1996, p 412.
142 Ibid, p 413.
143 Op. cit., Smillie, p 17.
144 See generally, Atiyah, P, *The Damages Lottery*, Oxford: Hart Publishing, 1997.
145 Ibid, p 193.
146 Wilkinson, R and Pickett, K, *The Spirit Level: Why More Equal Societies Almost Always Do Better*, London: Allen Lane, 2009.
147 Ibid, p 52.
148 Ibid.
149 Ibid, p 56.
150 Goodwin, E, 'Surgeon Criticises ACC Savings Drive', *Otago Daily Times*, 3 April 2010.
151 Ibid.
152 Ibid.
153 The National Health Service (General Medical Services Contracts) Regulations 2004 (UK), reg. 15(6).
154 The National Health Service (General Medical Services Contracts) Regulations 2004 (UK), reg. 2.
155 The National Health Service (General Medical Services Contracts) Regulations 2004 (UK), reg. 4.
156 Fehr, E and Gächter, 'Cooperation and Punishment in Public Goods Experiments', *American Economic Review* 90, 2000.
157 Ibid, pp 981–982.
158 Ibid, p 982.
159 Ibid.
160 Ibid.

161 Surowicki, J, *The Wisdom of Crowds: Why the Many Are Smarter Than the Few*, New York: Anchor Books, 2005, p 124.

162 See generally, Gilbert, J, *Breach of Faith, Breach of Trust*, New York: iUniverse, 2010; Brooks, B and Rizzo, A, 'Catholic Church: Shuffling Priests Around the Globe' *Buenos Aires Herald*, 18 April 2010 http://www.buenosairesherald.com/BreakingNews/View/30996; 'Trust in Catholic Church Plummets Amid Abuse Scandal' *The Local: Germany's News in English*, 24 March 2010 http://www.thelocal.de/society/20100324-26081.html; 'Pope Failed to Act on Sex Abuse' *BBC News*, 25 March 2010 http://news.bbc.co.uk/2/hi/8587082.stm; Pope Benedict XVI, *Pastoral Letter of the Holy Father Pope Benedict XVI to the Catholics of Ireland* http://www.vatican.va/holy_father/benedict_xvi/letters/2010/documents/hf_ben-xvi_let_20100319_church-ireland_en.html. Geoffrey Robertson in *The Case of the Pope: Vatican Accountability for Human Rights Abuse*, New York: Penguin, 2010, argues that the Pope (when he was Cardinal Joseph Ratzinger) covered up sexual abuse cases, and thus he should be prosecuted by the International Criminal Court.

163 World Medical Association General Assembly, *The World Medical Association Statement on Medical Ethics in the Event of Disasters*, Stockholm: World Medical Association General Assembly, 1994, clause 4.

164 Ibid, clause 1.

165 Ibid, clause 4.

166 Ibid, clause 3(4)(b).

Chapter 4

Complaints processes
A chance to build trust

The theory of distrust

External regulation of the healthcare profession is based on the premise that the profession cannot be trusted to deliver safe and effective healthcare without being watched over. The assumption is that, left to their own devices, healthcare professionals have too much power, with the temptation that such power may be misused. Legal systems have a process of checks and balances so that power is not all in one group's hands.[1] Parliament makes statute law, but interpretation of that law is left to a different branch of government, the judiciary. Another branch – the executive, such as the police – carries out the directives of the law. Through the process of democracy, citizens directly partake in deciding who will be in government, thereby providing a further check on parliaments that pass laws the citizens disagree with. The media provide a check on these processes by reporting on how they are carried out. The theory is that if everyone plays their role independently and fearlessly, then we can trust the system, because there is an equalising of power through the checks and the balances of each part.

The checks and balances theory, whereby power is separated and dispersed, requires constant vigilance and comes under pressure if one part becomes too dominant. For example, parliament can become too dominant if it decides to pass laws quickly and arbitrarily to assert its own authority. It may be some time before the correcting measure of voting comes into play. The executive, such as the police, may assert too much authority, particularly if encouraged by one of the other branches of government, and again it may take time before correction measures are put in place. The theory of distrust says that no system, whether it be a system of checks and balances or a system of benign authority, will in itself guarantee a culture of safe, effective and trusted outcomes: all systems must be subject to constant vigilance. All theories, if taken too far, can self-destruct. The problem with the theory of distrust is that it leads logically to more distrust. It says people cannot be trusted; therefore, we will constantly check on them. That does not make them any more trustworthy, just more watched. And who is to say the watchers are more trustworthy? Over the last

20 years in New Zealand, we have moved from a culture where healthcare professionals were trusted and left largely to their own self-regulation, to a situation where there are multiple pathways to complain about the actions of a healthcare professional.[2] The 'multiple pathways of the current complaints system in New Zealand' have been described as 'death by 1,000 arrows'.[3] There is the Privacy Commission, the Disciplinary Tribunal, the Human Rights Review Tribunal, as well as the Accident Compensation Committee and the Health and Disability Commission. Each one of them relates to the other, hence the idea of multiple arrows going from one external regulator to the other.

Complexity by itself does not mean the systems are necessarily broken. The intent behind all these processes is noble. The hope is that this external scrutiny will make healthcare professionals more accountable to their society, and thereby make healthcare safe and appropriate. The checks and balances of external scrutiny are assumed to build a climate of trust between the public and healthcare professionals. Regulation can become an end in itself; an all-powerful response that has unintended consequences, such as undermining the ability of healthcare professionals to practise at their best. This can lead to defensive responses and a lack of trust between healthcare professionals and patients. This lack of trust is evidenced by the studies discussed in this chapter of doctors who have been through complaints processes. The complaints process can be one of building trust, as this chapter will show, but the potential to destroy trust and confidence is strong. The problem is not all systematic; part of it is the perception the healthcare profession has of itself – one that has been bestowed on it – which is that of the healthcare professional as all-knowing. This perception blocks any attempt to equalise power between health professionals and patients, and thereby places a limitation on trust.

Complaint trends

The general trend in New Zealand, the United Kingdom and the United States has been for the number of complaints against healthcare professionals to increase. There is no systematic study to show why this is so. It could simply be that once there is a complaints process, it will be used in the sense of a self-fulfilling prophecy. This section speculates as to possible reasons for the increase in the number of complaints. The main purpose of this section is to show that an increase in the number of complaints actually provides more opportunities to build trust if the complaints are dealt with appropriately. Statistics from around the world show that, while there are a growing number of complaints against healthcare professionals, there is no consistent evidence that complaints are identifying problems that put patients at risk. It appears arbitrary when and where a complaint emerges.

A cross-sectional survey of New Zealand doctors randomly selected from registered general practitioners, registered hospital-based specialists and general registrants carried out by Wayne Cunningham, Raewyn Crump and

Andrew Tomlin showed a high and growing incidence of complaints in New Zealand.[4] According to the 2009 Annual Report of the Health and Disability Commissioner, 1,273 complaints were brought forth in 2006–2007, compared to 1,360 complaints brought in 2008–2009.[5] There are no reasons given by the researchers for this increase. It could be that there is more awareness of the complaints process or it could be that many patients are dissatisfied with the way they are treated.

International studies show a rise in complaints, but no consistent patterns for this upswing. The patterns in the United States are all over the map and they hint at the arbitrary nature of complaint. Navid Fanaeian and Elizabeth Merwin found that malpractice payment rates by doctors vary quite markedly between US states, from 0.73 per cent per physician each year in Alabama to 3.7 per cent per physician each year in Wyoming.[6] The difference has been argued to 'challenge the notion that the risk of malpractice litigation consistently promotes the quality of healthcare'.[7] William Meadow, Anthony Bell and John Lantos describe malpractice litigation in the United States as a lottery, in the sense that it is dependent on litigants and their lawyers rather than on any particular behaviour by the healthcare professional.[8] Examining doctors' impressions of the system, 80 per cent of them thought the claims that are brought are inappropriate, and that 80 per cent of situations where a claim would be warranted are not investigated.[9]

According to Zosia Kmietowicz, the rate of complaints to the General Medical Council in Britain rose by 50 per cent between 1999 and 2000.[10] Again, no reason is given for the increasing rate of complaints and the trend has continued upwards. According to the report *Data on Written Complaints in the NHS 2008–2009*, written complaints regarding general practice (including dental) healthcare services leapt from 43,942 in 2007–2008, to 48,597 in 2008–2009 – an overall increase of over 11 per cent.[11] The increase in complaints is likely to be because of a greater awareness amongst citizens of the complaints processes, rather than the healthcare profession lowering its standards. It may also be because healthcare is much more of a business now, and the pressure to be efficient and to deliver more for less means that less time is spent with individual patients. As a consequence, when things do not work out as expected, a complaint is laid as a means for the patient to be heard properly.

Wilhelm Kirch and Christine Schafii carried out a large-scale investigation at a German university teaching hospital to assess whether or not the advances in medical technology had reduced the frequency of misdiagnosis.[12] It is quite natural to think that with the progress of technology, there would be a corresponding reduction in the rate of misdiagnosis. A high expectation of better outcomes is logical. The study assessed diagnostic accuracy over a 30-year period and looked at 400 cases.[13] Misdiagnosis was defined in the study as when a 'disease that does not exist but is assumed to be present and when the failure to recognize the true existing disease leads to a worsened patient prognosis'.[14] Possible consequences of this incorrect diagnosis are 'either the omission of treatment or the initiation of incorrect therapy that may delay or prevent the patient's recovery'.[15] The researchers ultimately found that the frequency of misdiagnosis did not decrease and remains at a rate of 10 per cent, notwithstanding the improved quality of diagnostic technology.[16] Kirch and Schafii speculate that the lack of decrease may be due to 'misinterpreting and overestimating' what the new technologies and laboratory findings can provide and 'underestimating the classical clinical methods, such as the medical history and physical examination'.[17] Kirch and Schafii also point out that as elderly patients now live longer, they are more likely to develop multiple diseases, which makes diagnosis more complex.[18]

In 2000, the complaint rate per doctor per year in New Zealand was 5.7 per cent,[19] of which 85 per cent were dismissed.[20] Cunningham, Crump and Tomlin concluded that, taking the 2000 level as a base, 'almost one in every seventeen doctors will receive a complaint if they decide to practise medicine for another year'.[21]

In New Zealand, because of the Accident Compensation Act 2001, whereby compensation for injury caused by medical 'treatment' is paid by the state, litigation for personal injury suffered because of a careless or wrong act by healthcare professionals is statute barred.[22] Peter Davis and his fellow researchers examine whether the New Zealand no-fault system (whereby you cannot be sued in court for being at fault) increases the level of claims being made as compared with the 'low level of claims making traditionally associated with patient compensation under tort'.[23] They also discuss whether New Zealand's 'no-fault' system reduces social and clinical selectivity of patients' compensation claims.[24]

Davis and his fellow researchers found lower levels of claims making and receipt of compensation than was expected, despite the 'absence of financial and legal barriers' in New Zealand's no-fault system.[25] Their results were based on a sample of accident compensation claims for medical misadventure from the Auckland region in 1995.[26] As Davis and his fellow researchers state:

> On the assumption that 2 per cent of hospital admissions are associated with a compensable adverse event, approximately 3,000 such incidents would have been expected in the Auckland region for 1995. However, only about 150 such claims were filed, of which around two-thirds were successful . . . This low level of claims making and receipt is surprising, given the absence of financial and legal barriers.[27]

This low level of claims making is also supported by more recent statistics. In 2002, the Accident Compensation Corporation (ACC) received just 1,900 medical misadventure claims related to doctors, of which 480 were accepted and 53 were attributed to medical error.[28]

Davis and his fellow researchers found that lower levels of claims making were likely to be connected to the complexity of meeting the required definitions of medical misadventure, pain and suffering compensation being excluded from the accident compensation scheme, and the fact that hospital care is provided free of charge in New Zealand.[29] Davis and his fellow researchers ultimately conclude:

> Therefore, despite the apparent absence of procedural and financial barriers to making a claim for medical injury, the results of this study suggest that important processes of clinical and social selection are operating in the New Zealand system of no-fault compensation. This suggests that, without other procedural changes (such as patient advocacy, less complex compensation criteria, and a more straightforward claiming process), a move to a no-fault system does not necessarily of itself address issues of low and selective claims making and receipt.[30]

In New Zealand, DB Collins and CA Brown tracked the complaints made about medical practitioners from 1982 to 2005 and found a 'dramatic increase' in complaints during that time.[31] In 1982 there was a base figure of just over 100 complaints a year.[32] This increased to over 700 complaints in 2000.[33] The numbers levelled off to between 400 and 500 complaints per year between 2002 and 2005.[34] Exact population figures from 1982 are not available, but the 1981 New Zealand census puts the population at 3,175,737.[35] By December 2005, Statistics New Zealand estimated that the population had grown to 4,120,900, an increase of 29.76 per cent since 1981.[36] This moderate population increase was accompanied by a significant increase of between 300 and 400 per cent in the number of complaints against medical professionals.

Disciplinary hearings against medical practitioners have dropped equally dramatically during the same period, from a high in 1994 and 1995 of 91 per year, down to just eight in 2005.[37] Collins and Brown give three reasons for this drop.[38] Firstly, the setting up of the Health and Disability Commissioner's Office in 1995 enabled patients and family members to complain directly to the Health and Disability Commissioner, who would investigate and produce a report of its findings and provide recommendations on how to avoid similar problems in the future.[39] Health and Disability Commissioner reports do not have the force of law in the sense that they must be acted on. However, once they are released publicly, there is strong pressure to act. Their main advantage is that there is no cost to the private citizen who lodges a complaint with the commissioner. Once the report is released, the need for formal disciplinary proceedings reduces.

Secondly, the Medical Practitioners Act 1995 set up other ways of dealing with healthcare professionals who, in the past, would have been likely to go through disciplinary proceedings.[40] The Health Practitioners Competence Assurance Act 2003 has since replaced the Medical Practitioners Act 1995. The main vehicle of the Health Practitioners Competence Assurance Act 2003 is a system of competence assessment that authorises health practitioners' authorities to conduct competence reviews of individual practitioners, and create competence programmes for all its registered health practitioners, for a specified class of health practitioner or even for an individual health practitioner.[41] The 2003 Act also provides rehabilitation programmes for doctors who need up-skilling and more knowledge in particular fields. These programmes can include practical training or instruction in a particular area or undertaking a systematic process for ensuring that their services are up to the necessary standards.[42]

Thirdly, in 1998, the requirement that the ACC (which pays out compensation for treatment injuries) refers all findings it had made of medical errors to the Medical Council or Medical Disciplinary Committee was abolished, thereby lowering the possibility of disciplinary proceedings.[43] Complaint to the Health and Disability Commissioner is the preferred method of bringing medical misadventure and professional misconduct to external investigation in New Zealand.

Patterns of complaint

There is no consistent international pattern of which type of healthcare professionals are most likely to be complained against. In a study in Florida, John Ely and his fellow researchers found that more experienced doctors, with greater knowledge, were more likely to face malpractice claims.[44] However, in Michigan, Derek Weycker and Gail Jensen found that lower training qualifications and less experience were the key predictors of future claims for malpractice.[45] Cunningham, Crump and Tomlin found that general practitioners, male doctors and those with higher postgraduate qualifications carried the highest risk of complaint.[46] They speculate that the more experienced doctors are likely to be carrying the 'burden of responsibility for patient care' and are therefore more likely to receive a complaint.[47] The majority of complaints (over one-third of them), in the opinion of the doctors surveyed, were about an 'actual or perceived error in the practice of medicine contributed to the complaint being made'.[48] Cunningham, Crump and Tomlin fear doctors may view complaints as inevitable and 'thereby practise in such a way that error is minimised and their actions can be defended' – normally in a defensive manner, rather than in a manner that gives the patient the maximum opportunity for wellbeing.[49] Defensive medicine risks 'unnecessary investigation and over-referral, or . . . withdrawal of services'.[50] When the different perceptions of complaint between patients and health professionals are assessed, the potential to use the process to build trust becomes evident.

The perceptions of complaint

The only way complaints procedures can be understood is to see how they are perceived from different viewpoints. The key perspectives are those of the healthcare professional and the patient.

The healthcare professional's feelings of shame and guilt

Wayne Cunningham and Hamish Wilson argue convincingly that the epistemology of medicine is reliant on doctors 'knowing' and that failure to know may lead to a sense of failure of self, a sense of shame – 'a shamed person wants to hide, to withdraw, or to even disappear'.[51] The common perception and understanding of medicine is discussed by Cunningham and Wilson in the following terms: the healthcare professional, 'by applying correct medical understanding (history taking, examination and investigations), can "know" the best way to treat their patient's disease'.[52] This is an all-or-nothing philosophy that portrays the healthcare professional as all-knowing, which, of course, is a myth. No healthcare professional can be all-knowing. Not only is it impossible, but it also gives healthcare professionals too much power, and destroys any attempt to equalise power and build trust between healthcare professionals and their patients. It was the reaction to the all-knowing paradigm that led to the setting up of complaints processes in New Zealand. As discussed in the first chapter, Dr Green's assumption that he knew what was best for his patients led to the 'unfortunate experiment' of him not telling his female patients that they had cervical cancer in the hope that, by not treating it, the cancer would not get worse and the patients would recover.[53]

Not surprisingly, healthcare professionals who base their work on the all-knowing principle are devastated by complaints against them. Wayne Cunningham and Susan Dovey interviewed 10 general practitioners who had had a complaint made against them that did not proceed to an inquiry because all the complaints were dismissed.[54] They found that most of the doctors complained against, even though the complaints were not substantiated, had intense negative emotional responses after they received the complaint, such as stress, anxiety and anger as well as guilt and shame.[55] For example, a rural doctor had a complaint made about their attitude during a late-night call-out. The doctor described the patient as 'very demanding'.[56] After the complaint, the doctor reported feeling like a 'bad doctor' and experienced feelings of 'self-doubt'.[57] Many of the doctors in the study felt that complaints had knocked their confidence. A doctor who had a complaint made against them for their failure to diagnose a patient's illness said they felt that 'my decision-making process was slowed down. I began to lose a degree of confidence in my ability to assess the situation accurately, and to make proper medical decisions'.[58] Another doctor, complained about because of alleged improper conduct with a middle-aged woman, said, 'Something like this shatters your confidence, I suppose. It shouldn't, but it does.'[59]

We want healthcare professionals to learn from complaints so that they continually improve. If the process, particularly when complaints are dismissed, is leading to a lack of confidence and trust in a healthcare professional's own judgment, there is either something wrong with the process or the way healthcare professionals are reacting to it, or both. The consequence is that treatment standards are likely to drop in such an atmosphere.

Reactions to the doctor/patient relationship after a complaint were highly negative. The participants gave hostile comments about new and casual patients who complained. This is a worrying sign of blaming the patient because they are new, rather than listening to see if there is anything in the complaint that may inform the doctor about how they practise. Complaints by long-standing patients were reacted to with a feeling of being let down. A doctor who was the subject of a complaint about referring a patient with undiagnosed bleeding to a specialist colleague said that:

> You think you have a good relationship with somebody. It is partly the destruction of that that is so upsetting. It was that people that I'd cared for and liked should do that to me. That was really the most offensive thing.[60]

The word 'offensive' again shows an attitude of self-importance by the doctor, rather than any attempt to understand if there was anything to learn from the reason for the patient's complaint.

Loss of trust by the doctor for their patients emerged as a consequence of the complaint. A doctor who had been complained about for failure to diagnose, said about his patients: 'I found that I wasn't trusting them so much. I was looking at them thinking, "there is something hidden here" or, "they're not telling me something" or, "they're setting me up", you know.'[61] Such reactions are to be expected if a 'them and us' perspective is taken towards patients. A doctor who had been complained about because of improper conduct during a consultation with a middle-aged woman said:

> I think that the trust is still there for 95% of the people. But you're not quite sure who the other 5% are. Casual patients. They're much harder, aren't they? When a relationship is built up, they regard you as a person . . . A somewhat valuable person in their life.'[62]

Ultimately, trust is dependent on the personal relationships between the healthcare professional and the patient. Without mutual trust, the healthcare professional will not be focusing on what is best for their patient, but rather on how they can protect themselves against any future claims. The patient will be more reluctant to share information and the chances of a good diagnosis will diminish.

The all-knowing philosophy leads to blaming the patient who complains, rather than trying to understand *why* they might complain. A doctor who had been complained about because of their attitude towards a patient during a late-night call-out said, 'We're in a time where the doctor has very few rights and the patient has all the rights, and basically, we're there to be used and abused by the patients to a large extent.'[63] Patients are seen as the problem. When a patient with acute abdominal pain (severe stomach pain) complained about the way they were managed, the doctor said, 'He had some kind of antagonism towards doctors in general, maybe me in particular, and this was his chance. He wanted his pound of flesh from me for whatever reason.'[64] Patients who complain are categorised as 'wacky'.[65] For example, a doctor who was complained about by a patient's relative for being impolite and not supporting the complainant's belief that the patient was not being cared for properly by other members of the family, said, 'It's not very often a normal, reasonably intelligent person makes a complaint. It's always someone who's a little bit wacky.'[66] The complained-about doctors felt that patients did not understand the pressures they were under; as one of them said, 'You've got to be Mr Nice Guy all the time, no matter how much pressure is put on.'[67]

Cunningham and Dovey found that after a complaint against the doctors in the study, even when it was dismissed, the doctors 'referred earlier, investigated less, avoided "at-risk" activities such as emergency call-outs, and their decision making was based on avoidance of conflict with the patient'.[68] Cunningham and Dovey concluded that 'defensive medical practice' results from even unfounded complaints and that the process 'was so damaging to the GPs interviewed that the reverse of the assumed outcome (improved patient-care processes) resulted in every case'.[69]

The proposed solution here will look at both the process of complaint and the healthcare profession's perception of itself. The all-knowing healthcare professional model is part of the reason for the breakdown of trust between healthcare professionals and patients. How it does this is best understood by listening to how patients and their loved ones see things when medical error or other events do harm.

The patient's feelings of not being listened to and ignored

As Nancy Berlinger states in her book *After Harm:Medical Error and the Ethics of Forgiveness*, 'Upholding the principle of autonomy, of respect for the patient's integrity and dignity as a person and a moral agent, always means paying attention to the story a real patient is telling you.'[70] In the chapter entitled 'Patients' and Families' Narratives', Nancy Berlinger draws on the narratives of family members to reconstruct what it feels like to have lived through medical harm to someone they love.[71] Often, the loved family member has passed away because of the medical event. A strong theme that permeates the family stories is the feeling of not knowing what happened or why it happened, or being kept in the dark and stonewalled. The more things appear to be hidden or swept under the carpet, the more the family members are likely to feel the need to take things further, into a formal investigation of some kind. Lawsuits are explained as a way of 'finding out what really happened'.[72]

Roxanne Goeltz, whose brother Mike died in hospital in circumstances that were not fully explained, gave testimony to a United States Senate hearing on 'Patient Safety: Instilling Hospitals with a Culture of Continuous Improvement' on 11 June 2003.[73] Goeltz states:

> Mike is gone and we cannot understand what happened; the hospital has no explanation, no apology, no condolences, and no help to try and deal with the loss. Why are family members ignored, shunned and treated by the responsible facility as if they are at fault?'[74]

Goeltz's reaction 'was to get a lawyer, so we could get some answers'.[75] Lawsuits do not necessarily provide answers. Goeltz was told that there was 'no conclusive evidence of negligence', and that it would 'not be worth the work' the lawyer would need to do, so no civil action was taken.[76] Goeltz understood from her work as an air-traffic controller that medical errors can be explained as system failures.[77] What grieved and disturbed Goeltz the most was how no individual at the hospital came forward to explain what had happened and take responsibility for it.[78] Trust depends on individuals equalising their power, becoming vulnerable. Goeltz and her family wanted to achieve 'forgiveness in our hearts' but found it difficult 'when no one will face us whom we can forgive'.[79]

The story of Nancy Lim's death was made into a web documentary by her husband, Michael Barnes.[80] Nancy Lim, a nurse, had internal scar tissue from a previous operation. This scar tissue can bind to the intestines. Nancy experienced severe abdominal pain. A colleague suspected a bowel obstruction, whereby the intestines were being choked by the scar tissue adhering to them.[81] At the emergency room, Nancy and her husband told medical staff of the possibility of a bowel obstruction.[82] She was diagnosed as having gallstones and received little monitoring overnight.[83] She died the next morning because the scar tissue had strangled her bowel and this had led to septic shock.[84]

Families want understanding, most of all. They experience mistakes by healthcare professionals quite differently from the healthcare professionals themselves. For the family, the healthcare world is a strange, alien world that they do not understand. The event that has happened to their family member is the most significant and important thing in their minds at the time. This is all they can think about. Berlinger rightly argues that what families need most is knowledge – they need full disclosure of the mistake made and an apology for it, with the offer of fair compensation.[85] Such a process equalises power between the family and the healthcare professionals, which builds trust for future co-operation between the healthcare professional and the patient.

The Code of Medical Ethics of the American Medical Association (AMA) states: 'It is a fundamental ethical requirement that a physician should at all times deal honestly and openly with patients.'[86] A healthcare professional who perceives themselves as all-knowing may prefer to see what has happened as a 'complication' or that the patient was 'noncompliant', as pointed out by Berlinger, rather than confront their own limitations.[87] The combination of the all-knowing healthcare professional, whose identity is synonymous with their status, and the patient and the patient's family who want to know what really happened, creates a major trust gap between the two groups. If the family do not accept the healthcare professional's explanations, then the healthcare professional will blame the family for not understanding. The family will believe the healthcare professional is hiding something and not telling them what really happened. The stories of patients and their families that Berlinger uses as examples are all cases of highly articulate, well-educated people who are not easily fobbed off by the impersonal and partial responses given by the hospital authorities in each case. These are not people who believe that healthcare professionals are all-knowing, so bland bureaucrats or official statements from hospitals will not appease them.

Rebuilding trust

There are a number of ways trust can be rebuilt in the complaints process: trust of the public for healthcare professionals and trust of healthcare professionals for the patients. At the heart of this is Annette Baier's principle of trust – an attitude of wanting to equalise power, of empathy and understanding of the other.[88] In short, the ways of rebuilding trust are:

1   Changing the ways that healthcare professionals are perceived and how they perceive themselves;
2   Making disclosure, apology, repentance and forgiveness central to the process, rather than blame and punishment;
3   Simplifying and quickening the process;
4   Making structural changes that will reduce the opportunities and incentives for healthcare professionals to betray trust and to lose trust in their patients.

Healthcare professionals do not know it all

Healthcare professionals are given a monopoly to practise in their area of medicine on the basis that they have more knowledge and competence than anyone else in their particular field. It is not a big step to believe that they know it all, or at the very least that they should give the impression that they know it all. A brief trip through the history of healthcare will quickly disabuse us of this notion. Bloodletting used to be the order of the day to 'cure' all kinds of diseases.[89] What we would now call anxiety used to be thought of as a psychiatric condition. Large numbers of people who would have been put into institutions are today living safely in integrated and community-based care arrangements.[90] Lobotomies were thought to be the best way to deal with serious mental health conditions. Jay Katz, in his book *The Silent World of Doctor and Patient*, traces the history of the relationship between healthcare professionals and patients, which he describes as a 'history of silence'.[91] Katz says that, traditionally, '"Good" patients follow doctors' orders without question.'[92] Hippocrates is quoted by Katz as saying:

> Life is short, the Art long, Opportunity fleeting, Experiment treacherous, Judgment difficult. The physician must be ready, not only to do his duty himself, but also to secure the co-operation of the patient, of the attendants and of externals.[93]

As Katz points out, 'Sharing with patients the vagaries of available opportunities, however perilous or safe, or the rationale underlying judgments, however difficult or easy, is not part of the Hippocratic task.'[94] The history of the healthcare professional/patient relationship, which Katz carefully documents, shows that healthcare professionals are dedicated to their patients' physical welfare. This history emphasised the 'patient's incapacities to apprehend the mysteries of medicine and, therefore, to share the burdens of decisions with their doctors'.[95] Katz traces the history of Western healthcare back to the time of the ancient Greeks. It is no wonder that such a long history of the healthcare professional knowing it all cannot be turned around in one generation. It is deeply imprinted, to use the Freudian term, on the 'superego' of the healthcare profession.[96] There were exceptions in the history, such as Richard Cabot, who, in his 1903 essay, 'The Use of Trust and Falsehood in Medicine: An Experimental Study', expressed his strong belief that lying to a patient undermined trust.[97] Cabot's view was that a more honest relationship between patients and healthcare professionals would 'reinforce patients' confidence and the authority of the physician'.[98] Cabot's approach was not premised on giving patients more rights, but on the premise that because healthcare professionals had such authority, they should trust their patients to be able to comprehend the truth of what was happening. The Scottish psychiatrist Ronald Laing said, 'We all must continually learn to unlearn much that we have learned.'[99] No healthcare professional will ever be all-knowing: those who claim to be so are deluded. Not knowing is not failure by a healthcare professional; rather, it keeps the mind open to a range of possibilities, one of which may best explain what is happening to the patient.

Jerome Groopman, in his book *How Doctors Think*, says that a 'doctor's office is not an assembly line'.[100] Healthcare professionals need time to make the best decisions. Miscommunication is often the first detour away from a correct diagnosis. Healthcare professionals are reliant on patients telling them how they feel. Healthcare professionals must listen very carefully to what their patients say, and also listen to what the patient's relatives say about the patient's symptoms. At this stage, no healthcare professional can even begin to believe they know it all. Without the patient, and the patient's relatives if they are present, providing the clues, a misdiagnosis is possible. Groopman acknowledges that sometimes he would come to the end of his consultation and not be sure what to do next with a patient. He says in these moments he has learned to say to his patients, 'I believe when you say something is wrong, but I haven't figured it out.'[101] The patient will then be referred to another healthcare professional who will look at the situation afresh. Groopman has learnt to refrain from telling patients 'nothing is wrong with you' when they say they are still not feeling well.[102] In Groopman's words, to tell a patient nothing is wrong with them 'denies the fallibility of all physicians' and it 'splits the mind from the body. Because sometimes what is wrong is psychological, not physical'.[103]

Groopman cites the example of a businesswoman who told her doctor numerous times about pain in her breasts.[104] The mammogram results came back as normal but the woman continued to complain that she had aches in her breasts. Her doctor told her 'nothing is wrong with you'.[105] The explanation given by the doctor was stress. The woman went to another doctor who did further tests and diagnosed her with cancer. The woman's diagnosis was delayed by two years and by this time the cancer had spread to more than a dozen of her lymph nodes.[106] Even if the further tests had proved negative and there was no cancer, the diagnosis 'nothing is wrong with you' would not be helpful. Even if the condition was psychological, the patient still needs reassurance and treatment to deal with their psychological problems.

If trust is to thrive, the healthcare professional and the patient should not make any assumptions. Groopman cites a study of 45 doctors in California who were caring for a total of 909 patients.[107] Two-thirds of the healthcare professionals did not tell the patients either how long to take a new medication or what its side effects could be.[108] Just under half of the healthcare professionals failed to specify the dose of the drug and how often it should be taken.[109]

Even when pills are colour-coded, miscommunications can still happen. Different shades of the same colour can lead to confusion unless a careful check is made. Groopman cites the example of an elderly woman with an underactive thyroid who was not responding to treatment.[110] The patient had been told to take purple pills for the condition. It was subsequently found out, when she brought the pills into the doctor, that one pill containing 175 micrograms of thyroid hormone was one shade of purple, while the pill containing 75 micrograms was a slightly different shade of purple.[111] The patient was not able to distinguish the different shades of purple and hence the dosage.

Dr Groopman concludes his analysis in *How Doctors Think* by observing that he had, in the past, looked to 'textbooks and medical journals; mentors and colleagues with deeper or more varied clinical experience; students and residents who posed challenging questions' to improve his thinking about his patients.[112] But after writing the book, he now realised that he had a virtual mentor to improve his thinking – his patients or their family members or a friend who, 'with a few pertinent and focused questions, protect me from the cascade of cognitive pitfalls that cause misguided care'.[113] Dr Groopman says that 'by opening my mind I can more clearly recognise its reach and its limits, its understanding of my patients' physical problems and emotional needs. There is no better way to care for those who need my caring'.[114]

In 1964, Louis Lasagna, the Academic Dean of the School of Medicine at Tufts University, wrote what has been termed 'A Modern Version of the Hippocratic Oath', which has since become widely used in medical schools in the United States.[115] A paragraph in this oath reads as follows: 'I will not be ashamed to say "I know not", nor will I fail to call in my colleagues when the skills of another are needed for a patient's recovery.'[116] This is a strong concession to the all-knowing paradigm, which is partly self-generated and also expected by society. It is an essential ingredient of healthcare education and ongoing training that it is simply not possible to know it all. In fact, it is dangerous for patients when healthcare professionals have such an attitude. It is the opposite of equalising power and breeds distrust, whereas accepting limits and working with the patient as a party to solve the problems builds trust.

The case of Allan Smith, a 56-year-old victim of swine flu (H1N1 virus infection) who was admitted to New Zealand's Auckland Intensive Care Unit suffering from 'intractable pneumonia', graphically shows the risks of healthcare professionals thinking they always know best.[117] After Smith's hospital admission, the specialists taking care of him told his family that he was going to die and that he should be removed from the life-support system that was keeping him alive.[118] The family asked if Smith could be treated with megadoses of vitamin C.[119] The healthcare professionals were of the view that it would not make any difference to his health but, to placate the family, they administered two large doses (25 grams) of vitamin C.[120] After three days, Smith began to recover to the degree that he came off life support completely, even though he had received a further diagnosis of hairy cell leukaemia. The vitamin C was stopped and Smith's health deteriorated.[121] The vitamin C treatment was then begrudgingly resumed, against the doctors' wishes, at a lower dose (2 grams), after pressure from Smith's family.[122] Smith began to recover and was moved to Waikato Hospital in an induced coma. At the new hospital the vitamin C treatment was once gain stopped.[123] The family brought in a lawyer who warned Waikato Hospital that they were 'in danger of being in breach' of Right 7 of New Zealand's Code of Health and Disability Services Consumers' Rights (Code of Consumers' Rights).[124]

Right 7 of the Code of Consumers' Rights is the right to make an informed choice and give informed consent.[125] The emphasis in Right 7 is on the patient making an informed choice before services are provided.[126] There is nothing in the right that requires a medical service to be provided merely because the patient wants it. The lawyer was obviously persuasive and the hospital agreed to resume the treatment (at 2 grams of vitamin C per day), which led to a full recovery.[127] Eventually, when higher doses of vitamin C were given to Smith, he recovered rapidly. Smith walked out of hospital with all signs of swine flu, pneumonia and hairy cell leukaemia gone.[128]

The medical experts' view was that there is no hard scientific evidence to show that vitamin C could combat the swine flu virus. The fact that a high dosage of vitamin C had made an observable different to this particular patient showed that there were reasons to think that the swine flu virus was responding to the vitamin C in a way that may not be fully understood right now. The family's plea to continue with the vitamin C treatment was not based on a whim but on the experience of seeing Smith's health improve after large doses of vitamin C were administered to him. Even if there was no hard scientific evidence to show why this occurred, the fact that it did shows there will be situations where healthcare professionals, holding fast to knowing it all, can put a patient at risk of certain death. A mind open to all possibilities, realising the limitations of its knowledge, is the best way for trust to be fostered.

There is a rich and insightful literature on how cognitive errors can occur in diagnosis.[129] Jerome Kassirer and Richard Kopelman say that 'diagnostic errors are the consequences of inadequate knowledge, defective information processing, or some combination of the two'.[130] There are also cognitive biases that all humans are subject to. One is 'representativeness', where we make judgments based on close resemblance to other events we have experienced.[131] Kassirer and Kopelman cite an experiment whereby the personal attributes of an introverted and meticulous individual were described.[132] The participants were asked to say whether they thought the person was 'most likely an engineer, a physician, an airline pilot or a librarian'.[133] Most were confident the person was a librarian, based on classic stereotypes.[134] Another cognitive bias is the 'availability' mindset whereby we see matters through 'striking' situations we can recall from the past.[135] An experiment in which observers were asked to identify how many females and males there were on a list illustrates this error. There were in fact equal numbers of both sexes, but when disproportionate amounts of famous females or famous males were put on the list, participants guessed the list was not evenly split between the sexes.[136] A further cognitive bias is caused by 'anchoring', whereby the initial starting point influences the outcome.[137] Another classic experiment shows the consequences of this bias. One group was asked to 'estimate the product of $8 \times 7 \times 6 \times 5 \times 4 \times 3 \times 2 \times 1$ and another group was asked to estimate the product of $1 \times 2 \times 3 \times 4 \times 5 \times 6 \times 7 \times 8$'.[138] The average score of the first group was 2,250 and the second group's average answer was 512. The correct answer is 40,320.[139]

Pat Croskerry, who has written extensively on decision making in the healthcare context, surveyed 30 career emergency physicians about how much they had read about decision making as a discipline.[140] Whilst all thought decision making was crucial for their work, 97 per cent said they had not read about decision making.[141] Experience in a field is likely to lead to knowledge of pitfalls that can be avoided. Croskerry is of the view that learning about decision making and how to avoid biases can make for better decision making at an earlier stage.[142] It is worth a try. At the very least, it is acknowledging that no one can know it all. We can all be susceptible to bias if we are not constantly vigilant.

Make disclosure, apology, repentance and forgiveness central to the complaint process rather than blame and punishment

Disclosure

Disclosure simply means telling the truth about what happened. This is not likely if the consequences of telling the truth are punishment and legal action against the healthcare professional. Berlinger neatly summarises the devices used by healthcare professionals to deflect attention from the truth. Healthcare professionals have been known to say things like 'it was only a technical error', 'things just happen', 'the patient won't understand', 'the patient does not need to know'.[143] These deflections are perfectly understandable in a world where the healthcare professional's career and the institution's reputation are at stake. Self-preservation is a strong human instinct. It is easy to take the moral high ground when the blowtorch of professional humiliation is far away; more difficult when looking down the barrel of the fear of loss of status in a career that has been built on countless hours of sacrifice and hard work. Truth – which depends on how you look at it – is hard to find when the healthcare system encourages healthcare professionals to paper over the cracks rather than acknowledge them. The most that can be done here is to appeal to the reasons why disclosing the truth, as best one can, is the right thing to do. It is also the thing that is most likely to lead to trust and improving the situation for the future.

In a healthcare relationship, the healthcare professional is in the relatively strong position and the patient in the more vulnerable position, because the patient is unwell. The Hippocratic oath is an acceptance of this vulnerability when it instructs physicians to 'do no harm' to a person who is already in a weak and defenceless state.[144] If a healthcare professional does do harm, whether it be carelessly, inadvertently or through ignorance, the Hippocratic oath has been breached. The Hippocratic oath itself does not suggest that the harm caused has to be intentional, simply that doing harm is to be avoided.

Starting from a premise of doing no harm, and then harm being done, creates an obligation to rectify that harm. The first way to do that is to be honest with the patient as to how and why the harm occurred. To gloss over the harm, or to obfuscate, confuse and minimise it, is to create further harm. The desire to protect oneself is strong, but the Hippocratic healthcare professional must look at the world from the patient's point of view. The patient is the one who has suffered the harm; he or she is the one who needs to know how things have gone wrong. This does not mean the healthcare professional should admit they are at fault simply to make the patient feel better. The healthcare professional must first be clear about what has happened and their responsibility, or otherwise, for the problem. Only the healthcare professional can know their part of the harm caused, and they must not flinch from an honest assessment of the situation. This is not easy in a context where there are external pressures, such as those of the hospital where the health-care professional works, who will want to preserve their reputation. The most that can be asked is that when things go wrong, and a patient is harmed, the health-care professional involved will give the patient, as best they can, an honest assessment of how and why things ended up the way they did. This will be easier if there is a culture of forgiveness at the end of the process. Such a culture of forgiveness will only begin to flourish if healthcare professionals take the difficult first step of giving full disclosure as to what happened and why.

Apology

The conceptual problem with an apology is whether or not it is sincere. Was it given just to avoid more draconian consequences? Was it given as an easy way out? These questions can only be answered by the way the apology is given and what follows from it. An apology needs to make it clear that the person giving it is accepting responsibility for their actions, and not explaining them away in the guise of an apology. Berlinger provides an example of an oncologist who gave incorrect information to a patient about the stage of her cancer.[145] This information caused the patient to fear that her cancer might be far more advanced than she had been previously told.[146] Repeated attempts to contact the oncologist failed when there was no return of her calls. Eventually, a nurse told the woman that the information she had been given was incorrect, and that the oncologist had been aware of this but had still failed to tell the patient.[147] The oncologist finally did talk to the patient over the phone and merely said, 'I'm sorry, but I had 36 patients that day, and we mixed up your records with the other new patients' records.'[148] This did not relieve the patient's anguish as it showed no sense of accountability for what had happened. The oncologist knew he had not acted properly and that the patient would be in a state of high anxiety and fear because of the false information she had received. Yet the oncologist did nothing to alleviate the patient's pain until he had to, and then merely blamed his busy workload, rather than accepting any personal responsibility for the mistake. Relationships between patients and healthcare professionals are not healed by such an apology; if anything, they are made worse and trust goes out the window. The oncologist had made no attempt to understand what it might have been like for the patient and had made no attempt to equalise power. Therefore, there is no basis for further trust and, as Berlinger states, 'It became impossible for this patient to trust this physician.'[149] The patient is harmed twice; firstly by the bad advice and the failure to correct it, and secondly, by the insult that this was not really the healthcare professional's fault. An apology needs to be timely and to show good faith. The apology needs to be given directly to the patient, rather than through a third person, or through another medium such as phone or email. Apologies are difficult, but they are the most effective way of equalising power and starting the process of rebuilding trust.

Repentance

Repentance is an old-fashioned word in a world of performance indicators and rankings of who is the best. Repentance means to make amends for what has been done. Part of the amends is to acknowledge truthfully what has happened. If the cause was human error, which is inevitable no matter how many processes and checks we put in place – human beings make errors and always will – then repentance requires a combination of saying sorry, offering to do what can be done to make amends, reflecting on the error and trying to avoid it happening again. The corporate society we live in makes it difficult for repentance to occur. The corporate society's emphasis is on success and moving onwards and upwards, rather than on looking back and trying to make amends for things that have gone wrong. Doing this reeks of failure, a word not to be contemplated in the race for the top. Repentance is a wonderful opportunity to learn to see things as they really are, to be comfortable with our human weaknesses, rather than deluded by the hype of the rhetoric of endless success. It is a trite but true saying that we learn nothing from so-called success apart from perhaps to feed our ego for more success. Success always comes at a price, and the price is inevitably someone else's failure, someone else not doing as well. Success creates a hierarchy of achievement; it gives power to the so-called 'successful' and creates a gap between them and those who are not seen as being so successful. It is no wonder that those with that power do not want to lose it. Striving for success can lead to desperation, which we see most visibly in sport where athletes will risk long-term damage to their bodies in order to achieve success through the use of harmful drugs.

We learn far more from failure than from success. We learn that we are only human, that we are not all-knowing and all-powerful, and that we make mistakes, even when we are trying hard not to. Failure provides a wonderful opportunity to equalise power. We become as vulnerable as those we are supposed to be helping. Failure enables trust to be built, if we show the appropriate repentance.

In the section on disclosure, we discussed the example of the oncologist who caused his patient to fear that the stage of her cancer was much more advanced than it was. Instead of apologising straight away, repenting and providing the correct information immediately, the oncologist – who knew that the patient would be anxious – went on with his busy schedule and blamed his heavy workload for not getting back to the patient sooner. There is a cost to repentance. In this example, the cost would have been to interrupt the oncologist's busy schedule to talk with the incorrectly informed patient and alleviate her anxiety at the earliest opportunity, rather than the latest. Repentance involves taking action, not so that one will be forgiven, as that is up to the person who has been harmed, but because when harm has been done, everything possible must be done to alleviate that harm. Repentance means taking action because it is the best way to alleviate the harm that has been caused.

Berlinger cites the example of the Veterans Affairs Medical Centre in Lexington, Kentucky as an example of a fair compensation programme.[150] The programme was initiated partly as a reaction to the costs of unsuccessfully defending lawsuits where large awards were made against the hospital. More significantly, the hospital saw itself in a caregiver role, which extended beyond the aftermath of harm. The particular case that turned the corner for the hospital was one where a patient died because of the hospital's negligence, but the family were oblivious to this fact.[151] The hospital took the view that if they were to take the role of caregiver seriously, they must tell the family what really happened.[152] The main reason for the policy was that it was the right thing to do for their patients. It is also the right thing to repair the damage that has been done as fairly as possible.

In New Zealand, compensation is paid through the Accident Compensation Act 2001 whereby the loss is spread across all employers by way of a levy. A hospital or medical centre could show their repentance by acting quickly to minimise the damage. Compensation is money, but repentance also requires action by those involved: it may be by providing extra care; it may be by helping with chores around the person's house because they have had to spend more time recovering. It may be listening to the person who suffered harm and working with them to put in place processes that will avoid it happening to another patient in the future. As Berlinger puts it, 'Repentance after harm . . . requires direct engagement with the injured party and attentiveness to their stated needs.'[153]

Forgiveness

To err is human, to forgive divine.[154] Forgiveness is difficult. It cannot be demanded, nor can it be expected. It takes time, particularly if the harm is grave. If I were Nancy Lim's husband, I would find it very difficult to forgive the misdiagnosis of her bowel obstruction.[155] If Lim's condition had been correctly diagnosed, she would have lived. Instead, she was told she had gall-stones and received little monitoring.[156] I would want to know why the misdiagnosis happened. I would want to know how it could be avoided in the future, so that no one else had to go through the same pain and loss. I would have to work through my own human emotions of anger, frustration, futility and despair before even starting to contemplate forgiveness. Disclosure of what happened, and an apology for it, would go some way to helping with the journey to forgiveness. Berlinger talks of fair compensation. In the New

Zealand context, that would be covered by the Accident Compensation Act 2001 and could include rehabilitation costs, income compensation, lump-sum compensation, funeral grants, survivors' grants and spousal compensation.[157] I am not sure whether it is wise, or sensible, to put a monetary value on the loss of a life in terms of a lump-sum payment for what has been lost. There may be situations where the one left behind, because of their own health issues, may have been dependent on the one who has been lost. In these situations, it may be appropriate to compensate for that dependency. In most situations, it may well be better to accept that in the scheme of life, loss is inevitable and, short of people not being able to fend for themselves, to create an expectation of a large compensation scheme is likely to create a massive insurance industry based around that risk of compensation. It is much more likely to make it difficult for disclosure and apology to happen because of the potentially large financial consequences. It is also less likely to happen if the consequences are professional and public humiliation.

If we accept that human errors happen, as they do, and we want to encourage disclosure, apology, repentance and, hopefully, ultimately forgiveness, then the price to be paid is to remove the possibility of large financial payouts, and of public vilification when things go wrong, as they inevitably will from time to time. In cases where an injury can be put right or its impact minimised, then compensation would meet the costs of carrying out this work.

Simplifying and quickening the process

Justice delayed is justice denied. The longer a process goes on, the more deeply the grievance sets in. A study about the New Zealand justice system shows that delay is the biggest issue for those who responded.[158] With delay there are many costs. There are financial costs if legal advisers are involved. The longer the process, the longer some advisers will be involved and the greater the cost. There is the psychological cost of living with the possibility of no resolution. This cost affects all involved. There are the costs in productivity. While the matter is unresolved, the anxiety caused by it means that people do not function at the levels they are capable of. These are all the costs in not addressing the problem so that it can be dealt with in a way that makes it less likely to happen again.

A cross-section of 433 New Zealand doctors, which included general practitioners, hospital specialists and general registrants, were unanimous in their responses that complaints should be resolved rapidly.[159] One quote from the survey makes the point powerfully:

> Speed: In my situation I was devastated by the length of time it took to resolve. I contemplated suicide, leaving the profession, leaving New Zealand, etc. It was a very terrible time of my life and for years it was very difficult to talk about it.[160]

The doctors in the survey wanted responses to complaints to be rapid.[161] They wanted complaints to be dealt with in an environment where there was dialogue and mediation between complainants (and their advocates) and doctors (and their advocates).[162] They particularly wanted the system to be capable of seeking improved outcomes for the patient. This would be done by clearly pointing out where the failing had occurred – was it attributable to healthcare systems, errors in the practice of medicine, or to wrongdoing?

The longer any process takes, the more stress it places on everyone involved. The complainant has to live with the uncertainty of what the outcome may be, which leaves more room for resentment to build up. It is more difficult to look forward because the past has not been resolved or dealt with. It also creates stress for the healthcare professional against whom the complaint is made. They live with the uncertainty of what might happen. Anxiety and lack of confidence in one's ability to act would be natural reactions in such a situation. The healthcare professional's effectiveness levels are likely to drop, which is likely to put other patients at risk. The simplest way to quicken the process is to engage in open and honest disclosure right from the beginning when something has gone wrong.

If there is a genuine belief that the healthcare professional or the organisation are not at fault in any way, then it is important for an independent third party to investigate and assess the complaint straight away. If there is no basis to the complaint, it should be dismissed and then there would be no opportunity for uncertainty and stress to fester for too long. A simple procedure we have in New Zealand is a complaint to the Health and Disability Commissioner.[163] The Commissioner is then duty bound to investigate the complaint and write a report. The goal is to have the reports completed within two months. In 2009, this was achieved only 64 per cent of the time.[164] The main reason for this is that those who are complained against are given time to assemble and produce evidence and to gain expert testimony. This is because these reports, once released publicly, can have wide ramifications. The Health and Disability Commissioner only has power to declare a breach of the Code of Consumers' Rights, but no authority to provide a remedy to the complainant.[165] The Commissioner can recommend that the practitioner apologises to the complainant and make suggestions for improving future practice.[166]

The case of Dr Tom O'Flynn shows the impact of a report by the Health and Disability Commissioner that has had dire consequences.[167] Dr O'Flynn was the clinical director of the Southland Hospital's Mental Health Unit. One of the admitted patients was Mark Burton. Burton was released from the unit in March 2001 and then killed his mother in a frenzied attack, stabbing her 56 times and setting her alight in the family home.[168] Burton's father, Trevor, a former policeman, had sent a letter to the unit the day after his son was admitted to hospital, saying that he feared his son would harm his mother or brother.[169] Trevor laid a complaint with the Health and Disability Commissioner about the hospital releasing his son, when he had warned against it. It was alleged that the director, Dr O'Flynn, had failed to supervise Burton's primary doctor, a Dr Fisher. Dr Fisher was found guilty on 17 charges of professional misconduct for his poor care of Burton. The Health and Disability Commissioner found that Dr O'Flynn's work did not meet the standard of a clinical director.[170] Dr O'Flynn's unit was described in the report as 'lax and laissez-faire'.[171] These remarks were not specifically directed at Dr O'Flynn, but were general remarks about the operation of the mental health unit. As the director of the unit, Dr O'Flynn felt the comments were directed at him.[172] He said that the letter sent by Trevor about the risks of Burton being discharged never came to him, or to Dr Fisher.[173] He wished he had seen it. Nor had he seen a letter in Dr Fisher's home resources file raising concerns about his work.[174]

The Medical Practitioners Tribunal found Dr O'Flynn not guilty on charges of professional misconduct.[175] The Tribunal found he was working massive hours to plug the gaps in an understaffed mental health service. He had over 500 patients and was working the equivalent of two people's full-time jobs. The Tribunal's decision recorded that:

> Dr O'Flynn said that having dedicated 20 years of his life to working with children, adolescents and adults with mental health problems, and having fought against stigmatisation and prejudice (on behalf of his patients), he deeply resented being "misrepresented" in the HDC's report.[176]

After hearing Dr O'Flynn and many of the witnesses, the Tribunal was:

> unanimously and firmly of the view that Dr O'Flynn is deeply committed to the welfare of his patients and of all those patients who have access to the Service. We do not find any trace at all of "stigmatisation" or "paternalism" in Dr O'Flynn's philosophy or practice. Quite the contrary.[177]

The ultimate consequences were that Dr O'Flynn stopped practising because of the unfairness he had suffered. The Health Commissioner's report concluded that the 'overall impression' of Southland's District Health Board inpatient mental health service at the time was that there was a 'sense of complacency; a pattern of sloppy care that was lax and laissez-faire'.[178] This emotive and subjective language undermines trust. There is no problem with pointing out specific mistakes that can be learnt from and improved on in the future. This is how we all learn. But once we are accused of 'sloppiness' and 'stigmatising' others, and this accusation is made public, with no defence to it, then our ability to learn is compromised. The attack becomes directed at the personal integrity of a person, who the Health and Disability Commissioner acknowledges was:

> in an environment that is geographically isolated and short of psychia-trists and other skilled staff – was obviously complex and demanding and, at times, lonely. The Clinical Director had to shoulder a heavy work-load in part because of shortage of psychiatrists . . . he was working in an environment of constant time pressures.[179]

In hindsight, some members of the director's staff made decisions that turned out to be wrong. The consequences were the very sad killing of a mother by a son. The primary healthcare professional who made the decision to release Burton was found guilty of professional misconduct.[180] The judgmental language used against the mental health unit has not only undermined Dr O'Flynn's confidence, but also driven him from this work.[181] It is impor-tant to find out what went wrong and why, to avoid future repeat behaviour and thereby build trust for the future. Judgmental emotive slurs on the integrity of the unit as a whole, which on further analysis turned out to be untrue, destroyed the director's trust in the complaints process. It has the potential to destroy trust in the whole psychiatric care sector, which is called upon on a daily basis to make difficult decisions about those in its care. To be fair to the health and disability reporting process, the use of judgmental language is not common. Over 200 health and disability reports were read in preparation for this book. Generally, health and disability reports do acknowl-edge the context in which errors can occur, acknowledging how 'notoriously difficult' diagnoses can be in some cases and accepting how circumstances can limit choices.

With trust as the central value in complaints processes, the key steps would be, firstly, to be accurate in findings of fact and not to embellish them, and secondly, to be constructive in what can be done to rebuild trust when deci-sions have been wrongly made. Those writing the report on what happened should equalise power with the healthcare professional under scrutiny. Report writers should ask themselves: what was it like to be in the healthcare profes-sional's situation in those particular circumstances? This is not to excuse mistakes, but to understand them fully. Trust can be rebuilt by understanding the full context of a decision and working to improve that context. The sheer volume of work Dr O'Flynn had was an essential part of the context that needed to be addressed, rather than labelling his unit as 'sloppy' and 'pater-nalistic'. The O'Flynn case does show the need for the safety valve of a second opinion when unfair and unjustified criticisms are drawn. Unfair reports are less likely to happen if the mindset is one of clarifying what happened and why, with the ultimate goal of re-establishing trust in the healthcare system. Power is equalised when the person carrying out the investigation listens carefully to all sides, makes findings that are factually substantiated and not based on emotions, double-checks for accuracy and points to positive ways of preventing what happened from occurring again.

Structural changes to reduce opportunities to betray trust and incentives for healthcare professionals to create a trusted environment

Complaints processes are retrospective by nature. They can recommend changes that may prevent such an event happening in the future. An even better strategy is to think ahead, to think about why things go wrong. Sometimes they go wrong because people have character flaws. Such people, as Richard Abel says, 'have an extraordinary determination, and capacity, to rationalize misconduct'.[182] More education is not likely to work; behaviour is formed over time and being told to behave differently is not likely to work for people whose habits have been formed over a long period of time. Punishing such people may make us feel better but it is not likely to change their behaviour.

Dr Atul Gawande, in his book *Better: A Surgeon's Notes on Performance*, gives practical ways we can improve healthcare processes and prevent serious mistakes.[183] One of the most common errors in surgery is leaving swabs, sponges and other instruments inside patients. Punishing healthcare professionals after the event will not necessarily change this behaviour. It may help for a while, but old habits die hard. A better way to do it, Dr Gawande found, was to come up with a device that would track sponges and instruments so that it could be seen that some were still inside the patient.[184] This is not a 100 per cent foolproof solution, because it depends on the person operating the device to make sure that they turn it on and use it properly, but it is one way of eliminating a problem: a bit like putting a beeper on your car keys for when you put them down and cannot find them. Another example is the labelling of bottles. For example, '1.0' should be read as 'one' but, under pressure, could be read as 'ten', which would mean that you could accidently give a patient a 10-times higher dose than you meant to. This could be avoided by making the amount very clear in big letters, such as *one gram* emblazoned in bold lettering.

Environmental changes can also make a big difference. Dr Gawande points out that, as a surgeon in the operating room, he is meticulous about washing his hands thoroughly to avoid the possibility of infecting a patient during an operation.[185] But, once on the wards, he drops his guard from time to time and does not take the same degree of care over hand cleanliness. Dr Gawande gives the example of an engineer who designed the wards to be like the environment of an operating theatre.[186] Gowns and gloves, gauze and tape were kept at each bedside. Each patient had his or her own designated stethoscope. Stethoscopes used for one patient after another are notorious carriers of infection. A nasal culture was taken from each patient to see which of them carried resistant bacteria so that more stringent preventions could be used for them. Infection rates for the hospital fell by 90 per cent by changing the environment.[187]

The key is to keep looking for what works and what makes a difference. Tufts University nutritionist Jerry Sternin and his wife, Monique, were looking for solutions to the problem of malnourished children in villages in Vietnam.[188] The Sternins asked who had the best-nourished children in the village. They found there were some children who were well nourished, despite the poverty. The mothers of those children had found their own way, different from the accepted practice, to keep their children well nourished. They fed their children even when they had diarrhoea and gave them several small feeds each day rather than one or two large ones.[189] They added sweet-potato greens to the rice even though it was considered a low-class food to eat.[190] When the other villagers followed these practices, cases of malnutrition dropped by between 65 and 85 per cent in each village the Sternins visited.[191]

What worked was not a culture of compliance but what is called positive deviance, working out from within what works rather than being told from without. We must leave room for positive deviance to develop if we are going to create environments that work best for patients. We must trust that those who do the work, those closest to the action, as the mothers in Vietnam were with their children, will find ways to make their work better for their patients. Looking from the inside out is much more likely to create such an environment, rather than looking from the outside in. Governments and managers can never hope to fully understand what works best in healthcare relationships. Healthcare professionals and their patients will know this far better, based on their experiences. Imagine if every healthcare professional was thinking every day about ways to make the environment better for the treatment of patients. Imagine if every patient was spoken to personally about what did and did not work best at the end of their experience. We do not need rafts of internal audits and ranking based on outputs to create a more trusted and thereby a better healthcare world. We simply need to be always learning from every situation and giving the opportunity for those who know best, the healthcare professional and their patient, to be heard on what works best.

The Institute of Medical Committee on Quality of Health Care in the United States produced a report in September 1995 entitled *To Err is Human: Building a Safer Health System*.[192] The main findings of the report were that medical errors are not commonly caused by bad behaviour of individuals, but rather by processes and conditions that make mistakes more likely. An example given in the report is stacking patient-care units in hospitals with certain full-strength drugs even though they are toxic unless diluted.[193] This has resulted in fatal mistakes when drugs have to be accessed under time pressures. The environment should be such that it is easier to do the right thing under pressure. If the emphasis is on trust, then healthcare professionals need to be able to trust that the environment they work in enables them to avoid potential errors rather than create pitfalls. When errors do happen, they should be learnt from to avoid the same situation happening again. In an environment where building trust is the goal, incentives should be given to reveal mistakes and learn from them. This will be best achieved by giving legal protection to those who acknowledge mistakes and want to use them for the purpose of improving the environment for the future. Without legal protection from disciplinary procedures, there is no incentive to report mistakes and to improve systems.

The World Health Organization has carefully designed a surgical safety checklist to try and increase patient safety and reduce the possibility of mistakes.[194] A nurse reads out the checklist at three different stages: before anaesthesia, before the incision and after the operation.[195] The checklist addresses patient identity, surgery site and allergies, airwave obstruction and blood loss.[196] A key to the checklist is the trust it builds between members of the surgical team.[197] The surgeon, anaesthetist and head nurse each 'brief the team on any general issues that might be relevant'.[198] Research involving eight hospitals and 8,000 patients around the world was studied before and after the introduction of the checklist.[199] The rate of major complications fell by over a third, from 11 per cent of patients before the introduction of the surgical checklist, to just 7 per cent of patients after the surgical checklist was implemented.[200] Deaths reduced from 1.5 per cent of patients before the surgical checklist was introduced, to just 0.8 per cent of patients afterwards.[201] The key is not simply the checklist itself, but the fact that everyone in the surgical team counts as an equal and can raise issues if they think things are not right. According to Dr Gawande, who chaired the World Health Organization group asked to make surgery safer worldwide, and which ultimately developed the surgical checklist, the team checklist idea grew out of the airline industry.[202] In 1977, two Boeing 747s collided at high speed in fog on a Canary Islands runway, killing 583 people.[203] The captain on one of the planes had misunderstood instructions from air-traffic control and thought he had clearance to take off. The second officer had raised concerns but the captain disregarded them.[204] There was a checklist for take-off. The captain and second officer had not worked through it together so had not given themselves a chance to become a team and trust each other's judgment.[205] If there had been an equalisation of power, the accident would not have happened. Similarly, building trust between team members in an operating theatre protects the patients from error. Pat Snedden, the chairman of a Ministerial Quality Improvement Committee in New Zealand, said this about how the checklist gives everyone equal standing:

> If you think about power structures in the health system, it enables the lowest-ranking person to wave a flag if they think something's not right in the system. It gives them permission to do that. That's really important for the safety of the patient. It does not silence the voice that says, "Hang on, something's not quite right."[206]

Notes

1 See generally, Baron, C de Montesquieu, *The Spirit of the Laws*, in Cohler, A, Miller, B and Stone, H (trans.), Cambridge: Cambridge University Press, 1989.
2 The extension of the accident compensation scheme in 1974 to cover medical misadventure excluded negligence claims from the legal system. As a consequence, the sole legal avenue available to patients in the late 1970s and 1980s was through health professional board disciplinary proceedings. This system was criticised for its 'lack of independence, its secrecy, and its slowness'. Paterson, R, 'The Patients' Complaints System in New Zealand', *Health Affairs* 21, 2002, p 71.
3 Cunningham, W, 'The Medical Complaints and Disciplinary Process in New Zealand: Doctors' Suggestions for Change', *New Zealand Medical Journal* 117, 2004, Figure 1.
4 See generally, Cunningham, W, Crump, R and Tomlin, A, 'The Characteristics of Doctors Receiving Medical Complaints: A Cross-Sectional Survey of Doctors in New Zealand', *New Zealand Medical Journal* 116, 2003.
5 Health and Disability Commissioner, *Annual Report of the Health and Disability Commissioner for the Year Ended 30 June 2009*, Auckland: Health and Disability Commissioner, 2009, p 3.
6 Fanaeian, N and Merwin, E, 'Malpractice: Provider Risk or Consumer Protection?', *American Journal of Medicine Quality* 16, 2001, p 43.
7 Ibid.
8 Meadow, W, Bell, A and Lantos, J, 'Physicians' Experience With Allegations of Medical Malpractice in the Neonatal Intensive Care Unit,' *Paediatrics* 99, 1997, p e10.
9 Ibid.
10 Kmietowicz, Z, 'Complaints Against UK Doctors Rise 50 Per Cent,' *British Medical Journal* 322, 2001, p 448.
11 The Health and Social Care Information Centre, 'Data on Written Complaints in the NHS 2008-2009' (2009), The Information Centre for Health and Social Care http://www.ic.nhs.uk/statistics-and-data-collections/audits-and-performance/complaints/data-on-written-complaints-in-the-nhs-2008-09.
12 Kirch, W and Schafii, C, 'Misdiagnosis at a University Hospital in 4 Medical Eras: Report on 400 Cases', *Medicine* 75, 1996, pp 29–40.
13 Ibid.
14 Ibid.
15 Ibid.
16 Ibid.
17 Ibid.
18 Ibid.
19 Op. cit., Cunningham, Crump and Tomlin, p 7
20 Ibid.
21 Ibid.
22 Accident Compensation Act 2001, ss 32 and 33.
23 Davis, P *et al*, 'Compensation for Medical Injury in New Zealand: Does "No-Fault" Increase the Level of Claims Making and Reduce Social and Clinical Selectivity?', *Journal of Health Politics, Policy and Law* 27, 2002, p 834.
24 Ibid, p 835.
25 Ibid, p 850.
26 Ibid, p 837.
27 Ibid, p 850.
28 Op. cit., Cunningham, Crump and Tomlin, p 1.
29 Op. cit., Davis *et al*, p 850.

30 Ibid, pp 851–852.
31 Collins, D and Brown, C, 'The Impact of the Cartwright Report upon the Regulation, Discipline and Accountability of Medical Practitioners in New Zealand', *Journal of Law and Medicine* 16, 2009, p 596.
32 Ibid.
33 Ibid.
34 Ibid.
35 Department of Statistics, *New Zealand Official Yearbook 1982*, Wellington: Department of Statistics, 1982, p 55.
36 Statistics New Zealand, 'National Population Estimates: December 2005 Quarter' (2006) http://www2.stats.govt.nz/domino/external/pasfull/pasfull.nsf/web/Media + Release + National + Population + Estimates + December + 2005 + quarter?open.
37 Op. cit., Collins and Brown, p 597.
38 Ibid, pp 597–598.
39 See generally, Health and Disability Commissioner Act 1994, Part 4.
40 The Health Practitioners Competence Assurance Act 2003 has since replaced the Medical Practitioners Act 1995. The Health Practitioners Competence Assurance Act 2003 carries forward all of the major concepts of the Medical Practitioners Act 1995 but now applies them, where appropriate, not just to doctors but to a wide range of healthcare professionals.
41 Health Practitioners Competence Assurance Act 2003, s 40.
42 Health Practitioners Competence Assurance Act 2003, s 41.
43 Op. cit., Collins and Brown, p 598.
44 See generally, Ely, J *et al*, 'Malpractice Claims Against Family Physicians: Are the Best Doctors Sued More?', *Journal of Family Practice* 48, 1999.
45 Weycker, D and Jensen, G, 'Medical Malpractice Among Physicians: Who Will be Sued and Who Will Pay?', *Health Care Management Science* 3, 2000.
46 Op. cit., Cunningham, Crump and Tomlin, p 7.
47 Ibid, p 8.
48 Ibid.
49 Ibid.
50 Ibid. See also, Summerton, N, 'Trends in Negative Defensive Medicine Within General Practice', *British Journal of General Practice* 50, 2000.
51 Cunningham, W and Wilson, H, 'Shame, Guilt and the Medical Practitioner', *New Zealand Medical Journal* 116, 2003, p 1.
52 Ibid, p 2.
53 See generally, Cartwright, S, *The Report of the Cervical Cancer Inquiry 1988*, Auckland: Government Printing Office, 1988.
54 Cunningham, W and Dovey, S, 'The Effect on Medical Practice of Disciplinary Complaints: Potentially Negative for Patient Care', *New Zealand Medical Journal* 113, 2000.
55 Ibid, p 465.
56 Ibid.
57 Ibid.
58 Ibid.
59 Ibid.
60 Ibid.
61 Ibid.
62 Ibid, p 466.
63 Ibid.
64 Ibid.
65 Ibid.

66 Ibid.
67 Ibid.
68 Ibid.
69 Ibid, p 467.
70 Berlinger, N, *After Harm: Medical Error and the Ethics of Forgiveness*, Baltimore: Johns Hopkins University Press, 2005, p 4.
71 Ibid, pp 28–39.
72 Ibid, p 33.
73 Roxanne Goeltz's experience was first published within a National Patient Safety Foundation newsletter in 2000. Goeltz's testimony later became part of the United States Senate Hearing, 'Patient Safety: Instilling Hospitals with a Culture of Continuous Improvement', 11 June 2003.
74 Op. cit., Berlinger, p 33.
75 Ibid.
76 Ibid, pp 33–34.
77 Ibid, p 34.
78 Ibid.
79 Goeltz, R, 'For My Brother', *National Patient Safety Foundation Newsletter* 3, 2000, p 8. Discussed in Berlinger, op. cit., p 34.
80 Michael Barnes hosted this web documentary on the website, 'Blunt Instruments: Medicine, Law and the Death of Nancy Lim', formerly at http:www.nancylim.org. This website was discontinued in 2008; however, its contents are discussed in Berlinger, op. cit., pp 35–37.
81 Op. cit., Berlinger, p 35.
82 Ibid.
83 Ibid.
84 Ibid.
85 Op. cit., Berlinger, pp 38–39.
86 American Medical Association, 'Opinion 8.12 – Patient Information', *Code of Medical Ethics*, March 1981.
87 Op. cit., Berlinger, p 41.
88 See generally, Chapter II of this book and Baier, A, *Moral Prejudices: Essays on Ethics*, Cambridge: Harvard University Press, 1994, pp 180–181.
89 See generally, Kuriyama, S, 'Interpreting the History of Bloodletting', *Journal of the History of Medicine and Allied Sciences* 50, 1995, pp 11–46.
90 Brunton, W, 'The Origins of Deinstitutionalisation in New Zealand', *Health and History* 5, 2003, p 77.
91 Katz, J, *The Silent World of Doctor and Patient*, New York: Free Press, 1984, p 1.
92 Ibid.
93 Ibid.
94 Ibid.
95 Ibid, p 28.
96 Freud, S, *New Introductory Lectures in Psycho-Analysis*, London: The Hogarth Press, 1977. Discussed in Katz, op. cit., p 28.
97 Cabot, R, 'The Use of Truth and Falsehood in Medicine: An Experimental Study', *American Medicine* 5, 1903, 344. Discussed in Katz, op. cit., pp 25–26.
98 Op. cit., Katz, p 26.
99 Laing, R, *The Politics of the Family, and Other Essays*, London: Routledge, 1998, p 42.
100 Groopman, J, *How Doctors Think*, Melbourne: Scribe Publications, 2007, p 268.
101 Ibid, p 264.
102 Ibid.
103 Ibid.

104 Ibid, p 265.
105 Ibid.
106 Ibid.
107 Ibid, p 86. Taken from Tarn, D *et al*, 'Physician Communication When Prescribing New Medications', *Archives of Internal Medicine* 166, 2006, pp 1855–1862.
108 Op. cit., Groopman, p 265.
109 Ibid.
110 Ibid, p 267.
111 Ibid.
112 Ibid, p 268.
113 Ibid, pp 268–269.
114 Ibid, p 269.
115 Quoted in Sox, H, 'The Ethical Foundations of Professionalism: A Sociologic History', *Chest: Official Publication of the American College of Chest Physicians* 131, 2007, p 1540.
116 Ibid.
117 Gillett, G, 'Doctor Does Not Always Know Best' *Otago Daily Times*, 16 September 2010.
118 Ibid.
119 Ibid.
120 Ibid.
121 Ibid.
122 Ibid.
123 Ibid.
124 Ibid.
125 See generally, Right 7 of the Code of Health and Disability Services Consumers' Rights as prescribed by the Health and Disability Commissioner (Code of Health and Disability Services Consumers' Rights) Regulations 1996.
126 Right 7 of the Code of Health and Disability Services Consumers' Rights. For an introductory discussion of informed consent in New Zealand see Skegg, P, 'Consent to Treatment: Introduction', in Skegg, P and Paterson, R (eds), *Medical Law in New Zealand*, Wellington: Brookers Ltd., 2006, pp 145–169.
127 Op. cit., Gillett.
128 Ibid.
129 See generally, Schwartz, A and Elstein, A, 'Clinical Reasoning in Medicine' in Higgs, J *et al* (eds), *Clinical Reasoning in the Health Professions*, 3rd edition, Sydney: Elsevier, 2008; Kirch, W and Schafii, C, op. cit., pp 29–40; Kassirer, J and Kopelman, R, 'Cognitive Errors in Diagnosis: Instantiation, Classification, and Consequences', *The American Journal of Medicine* 86, 1989, pp 433–441; Croskerry, P, 'The Importance of Cognitive Errors in Diagnosis and Strategies to Minimize Them', *Academic Medicine* 78, 2003, pp 775–780; Croskerry, P, 'Achieving Quality in Clinical Decision Making: Cognitive Strategies and Detection of Bias', *Academic Emergency Medicine* 9, 2002, pp 1184–1204; Croskerry, P, 'The Theory and Practice of Clinical Decision-Making', *Canadian Journal of Anaesthesia* 52, 2005, pp R1–R8; Redelmeier, D, 'The Cognitive Psychology of Missed Diagnoses', *Annals of Internal Medicine* 142, 2005, pp 115–120; Hayward, R *et al*, 'Sins of Omission: Getting Too Little Medical Care May Be the Greatest Threat to Patient Safety', *Journal of General Internal Medicine* 20, 2005, pp 686–691; Gandhi, T *et al*, 'Missed and Delayed Diagnoses in the Ambulatory Setting: A Study of Closed Malpractice Claims', *Annals of General Medicine* 145, 2006, pp 488–496.
130 Op. cit., Kassirer and Kopelman, p 438.

131 Ibid, p. 439. Taken from Kahneman, D and Tversky, A, 'Subjective Probability: A Judgment of Representativeness', *Cognitive Psychology* 3, 1972, pp 430–454.
132 Op. cit., Kassirer and Kopelman, p 439
133 Ibid.
134 Ibid.
135 Ibid. Taken from Tversky, A and Kahneman, D, 'Availability: A Heuristic for Judging Frequency and Probability', *Cognitive Psychology* 4, 1973, pp 207–232.
136 Ibid.
137 Ibid. Taken from Kahneman, D, Slovic, P and Tversky, A (eds), *Judgment Under Uncertainty: Heuristics and Biases*, Cambridge: Cambridge University Press, 1982.
138 Ibid.
139 Ibid.
140 Croskerry, P, 'The Theory and Practice of Clinical Decision-Making', *Canadian Journal of Anaesthesia* 52, 2005.
141 Ibid, p. R3.
142 Ibid, p. R2.
143 Op. cit., Berlinger, p 41.
144 Hippocrates, 'Epidemics', in Jones, W (trans.), *Hippocrates Volume I*, Cambridge: Harvard University Press, 1948, p 165.
145 Op. cit., Berlinger, pp 59–60.
146 Ibid, p 59.
147 Ibid, p 60.
148 Ibid.
149 Ibid, p 60.
150 Ibid, p 69.
151 Ibid.
152 Ibid.
153 Ibid, p 80.
154 Pope, A, *An Essay on Criticism*, 1709.
155 As discussed in Berlinger, op. cit., pp 35–37.
156 Ibid, p 35.
157 Accident Compensation Act 2001, s 69.
158 Henaghan, M and Righarts, S, 'Public Perceptions of the New Zealand Court System: An Empirical Approach to Law Reform', *Otago Law Review* 12, 2010, p 342.
159 Cunningham, W, 'The Medical Complaints and Disciplinary Process in New Zealand: Doctors' Suggestions for Change', *New Zealand Medical Journal* 117, 2004.
160 Ibid, p 5.
161 Ibid.
162 Ibid, p 6.
163 See generally, Health and Disability Commissioner Act 1994, Part 4.
164 Health and Disability Commissioner, *Annual Report of the Health and Disability Commissioner for the Year Ended 30 June 2009*, op. cit., p 50.
165 Ibid.
166 Ibid.
167 Health and Disability Commissioner, *Southland District Health Board Mental Health Services: February–March 2001*, Invercargill: Health and Disability Commissioner, 2002; *Director of Proceedings v Thomas Paul O'Flynn*, Medical Practitioners Disciplinary Tribunal, 291/03/110D 15 July 2004 www.mpdt.org.nz/decision-sorders/precis/03110d.asp.
168 Henzell, D, 'The Good Doctor with a Damaged Reputation', *Sunday Star Times* 25 July 2004, p A8.
169 Ibid.

170 Health and Disability Commissioner, *Southland District Health Board Mental Health Services: February–March 2001*, op cit., p 86.
171 Ibid, p 107.
172 Op. cit., Henzell, p A8.
173 Ibid.
174 Ibid.
175 Op. cit., *Director of Proceedings v Thomas Paul O'Flynn*.
176 Ibid, at [580].
177 Ibid, at [586].
178 Health and Disability Commissioner, *Southland District Health Board Mental Health Services: February–March 2001* op. cit., p 107.
179 Ibid, p 85.
180 Op. cit., Henzell, p A8.
181 Ibid.
182 Abel, R, 'Restoring Trust', in *Lawyers in the Dock*, New York: Oxford University Press, 2008, p 512.
183 Gawande, A, *Better: A Surgeon's Notes on Performance*, London: Profile Books Ltd, 2007.
184 Ibid, p 255.
185 Ibid, pp 20–23.
186 Ibid, pp 23–24.
187 Ibid, p 24.
188 Ibid, pp 24–25.
189 Ibid, p 25.
190 Ibid.
191 Ibid.
192 Institute of Medicine, *To Err is Human: Building a Safer Health System*, Washington: National Academy Press, 2000.
193 Ibid, p 194.
194 World Health Organization, 'Surgical Safety Checklist' (2009) Safe Surgery Saves Lives www.who.int/patientsafety/safesurgery/en/.
195 Laugesen, R, 'Just Checking' *New Zealand Listener* 3643, 2010, p 18.
196 Ibid.
197 Ibid.
198 Ibid.
199 Haynes, A *et al*, 'A Surgical Safety Checklist to Reduce Morbidity and Mortality in a Global Population' *The New England Journal of Medicine* 360, 2009.
200 Ibid, p 491.
201 Ibid.
202 Laugesen, R, 'Flying Blind', *New Zealand Listener* 3643, 2010, p 21.
203 Ibid.
204 Ibid.
205 Ibid,
206 Op. cit., Laugesen, R, 'Just Checking', p 20.

Chapter 5

What happens when trust breaks down?

Breakdown of trust between healthcare professionals

Healthcare professionals often have to work together. If there is to be trust in these collaborations, it is crucial that each professional equalises power with the other professionals. Without trust, information is less likely to be shared openly, which will most likely be to the detriment of patients. Without trust, the opportunity to see the limits of one's own expertise and the appropriateness of another's expertise is less likely to happen, which again will put patients at greater risk.

The emphasis in the New Zealand Code of Health and Disability Services Consumers' Rights (Code of Consumers' Rights) on consumers and providers gives every consumer the 'right to co-operation among providers to ensure quality and continuity of services'.[1] There is nothing in the Code of Consumers' Rights to say that healthcare professionals must work together for the benefit of the patient.

In New Zealand, obstetricians and midwives, the healthcare professionals who used to work together for the good of pregnant women, have been fighting what has been described as a 'turf war'.[2] Trust has broken down between the two healthcare professions, who appear to have what has been described as 'almost diametrically opposing views of childbirth'.[3] Midwives place strong emphasis on protecting women from unnecessary medical intervention. Their emphasis is on allowing the natural process of labour to occur. Obstetricians protect women by using medical means such as caesarean sections to prevent risks to them and their unborn children. The former Health and Disability Commissioner, Ron Paterson, is cited as describing the difference as obstetricians taking a 'risk-averse, interventionist approach' and midwives 'a less-interventionist approach, to allow the normal physiological process of labour to proceed'.[4] In the 1990s, New Zealand carried out maternity reforms based on the idea that midwives should handle births where little or low intervention is anticipated, and that where there were complications, the patient should be handed over to an obstetrician.[5] If both professions trusted each other and were prepared to equalise power by seeing the benefits of each other's approach, they could have complemented each other for the good of the patient. However, communication broke down between the professions when they could not reach agreement on issues such as the appropriate time to hand over a patient's care from a midwife to an obstetrician. This is not surprising, given the language used on both sides to describe the other profession. Joan Donley, a leading midwife, is quoted as describing obstetricians as 'generals in the war against normal childbirth', and saying that 'the medicalisation of birth is a form of aggression and violence'.[6]

The Royal Australian and New Zealand College of Obstetricians and Gynaecologists made a submission in 2008 to the Australian government about the midwife-led maternity system in New Zealand, which means that midwives are in charge of 80 per cent of the births in New Zealand. The submission said:

> The New Zealand maternity system has been hailed by some as having introduced great benefits to the women of New Zealand. That is not a view held by this College. In summary, the New Zealand maternity reforms could in the future be viewed as 'an unfortunate experiment'.[7]

The submission goes on to say that the 'experiment' is responsible for raising infant and maternal death rates.[8] In short, it is portrayed as a disaster. The term 'unfortunate experiment' was upsetting for midwives because that was the term associated with 'the 1980s exposé into the cervical cancer scandal at National Women's Hospital and the words have became [sic] synonymous with a woman's loss of power over her own body, specifically at the hands of gynaecologists'.[9] Essentially, the words 'unfortunate experiment' are associated with women being disempowered by the medical profession, particularly gynaecologists.[10]

A major review into maternity services in Wellington, New Zealand found 'fundamental differences in the approach of obstetricians and midwives to management of a normal labour'.[11] The result was a lack of trust between the two professions, which meant that the communication required between obstetricians and midwives 'may not occur when it is needed to ensure the safety of mother and baby'.[12] The Wellington Maternity Services Review found an 'alarming' inability of obstetricians and midwives 'to work in a collaborative and supportive professional relationship with the other'.[13] The review concluded: 'There is a lack of respect, collegiality and collaboration between the obstetric and midwifery colleges that is reflected in some very poor relationships between individual midwives and obstetricians.'[14] There is no attempt to equalise power between the two professions. There is no effort to understand the other profession's point of view; just a desire to be right at the expense of building trust.

The battle lines between obstetricians and midwives were drawn across the whole of New Zealand. The consequence was that patients suffered and paid the price when trust between healthcare professionals broke down. A baby boy died during a breech delivery in Queen Mary Hospital in Dunedin.[15] As a result of the death, the midwife, Jennifer Crawshaw, was charged with manslaughter.[16] The basis of the charge was that the midwife had failed in her duty to the patient by allowing an unsafe natural breech birth to proceed. The jury acquitted the midwife.[17] This was largely because the mother of the baby boy gave her full support to the midwife. The mother accepted that she had been fully informed of the risks of a natural breech birth, but she had decided to proceed without medical intervention.[18]

Evidence given during the trial shows how an environment of mistrust had been created and how it affected decision making. The father of the baby, in response to a question that his wife was being pushed into having a caesarean section by the medical clinicians, said, 'Yes, that's correct.'[19] The father gave evidence that he and his wife were concerned by the fact that each time they went to the hospital, they saw a different clinician and they were unable to establish empathy with any of their clinicians.[20] The father concluded his evidence about the relationship with the medical clinicians by stating that he was 'very disillusioned'.[21] The mother of the child gave evidence that the medical clinicians were steering her towards a caesarean section with no other options, whereas the midwife, Jenny Crawshaw, preferred for the patient to make up her own mind about the advice she received from her and the clinicians.[22] It is not surprising in this environment, with the midwife listening to the patient and giving the patient choices, that the patient preferred the advice of the midwife to have the child naturally. Trust in the medical clinicians had ended for the mother and father.

Because trust between the midwives and obstetricians had broken down, the evidence showed that Jenny Crawshaw, the midwife who delivered the baby, asked the co-ordinator of the delivery suite if she could 'keep a secret', because 'she had a lady in the room having a first baby with breech presentation and wanted to do a vaginal birth and she didn't want anyone to know she was there'.[23] The co-ordinator of the delivery suite said that, 'Breech is not a normal presentation. Normally the medical staff would be involved.'[24] The reason given by the midwife for not wanting the medical staff to know was that the mother 'had made a decision and didn't want to have any further discussions with medical staff'.[25]

The gynaecologist on duty at the time the child died agreed in cross-examination that, prior to the birth, there had been a number of incidents involving arguments between obstetricians and midwives at Queen Mary Hospital in Dunedin.[26] It was agreed in cross-examination that obstetricians had gone into birthing suites uninvited, which had caused considerable tension for midwives carrying out deliveries and for women giving birth.[27]

This was the context in which the midwife, Jenny Crawshaw, asked the co-ordinator of the delivery suite, who was a registered nurse and midwife, to keep a 'secret' so that no medical clinicians would come into the delivery suite. The paediatric registrar on duty gave evidence that where a breech birth was likely to occur, or was occurring, it would be 'standard practice to have a paediatric person in attendance'.[28] The specialist obstetrician and gynaecologist who was on call on the day in question said she was 'devastated' when she was told that a breech birth was taking place without her knowledge and that the co-ordinator knew it was taking place all along.[29] The specialist said, 'I felt the poor outcome for baby and mother could have been avoided if I had been allowed to see the mother first.'[30] The midwifery director for the Queen Mary Hospital in Dunedin gave evidence that the midwife, Jenny Crawshaw, did not want the specialist on-call obstetrician/gynaecologist to know about the breech birth because she 'would have done a caesarean section'.[31]

Senior lecturers in neonatology and midwifery gave evidence that anticipation of risk is important and that this is best done by making people available in advance. The midwifery lecturer said that, 'because the midwife was so overt about not calling the obstetric assistance, even quite late in the birth, despite all the risk factors and the clear recordings she had taken which showed it was, her actions were grossly negligent'.[32] It is hard to believe that a dedicated midwife who is strongly focused on her patient's interests would end up in this situation. An answer by the midwife, Jenny Crawshaw, under cross-examination explains it all:

> Unfortunately at Queen Mary at that time there was a lot of tension and there had been occasions when obstetricians had shouted at midwives and occasions, one specific occasion not long before that, where the obstetrician had overruled the woman's wishes and barged into the room. And in the context of that, asking for advice became very complex.[33]

Former Health and Disability Commissioner Ron Paterson, who carried out an investigation into this case, asked Jenny Crawshaw why she did not at least have specialists on standby. Her reply was that 'given the history of stand-up arguments between midwives and obstetricians in the corridors of Queen Mary and the climate that was prevalent, it was simply not realistic to have obstetricians/paediatricians on standby'.[34] Crawshaw's reply was based on her belief that the obstetricians would have either insisted on full involvement, which the mother did not want, or they would have refused to participate because they were not allowed to be fully involved. This case highlights the importance of co-operation and communication between members of the healthcare profession. As one of the experts at the criminal trial said, 'Co-operation, collaboration between colleagues, midwifery and medical is an essential part of the delivery of high quality obstetric care, in my view.'[35]

In another review, carried out by the Health and Disability Commissioner in June 2008, midwives and obstetricians took different views of the outcome. A boy suffered oxygen deprivation and died of brain injuries. The mother was transferred too late from a rural birthing unit to a hospital. The midwifery expert for the review described the midwife's treatment as 'reasonable' and 'close and appropriate'.[36] The obstetric expert said the opposite: 'By any first world standard, the care in this case is below what is generally considered acceptable.'[37]

A coroner's report, which investigated the death of a baby girl after a home breech birth, recommended a review of the rights of the unborn child.[38] The mother had chosen to proceed with a home birth despite being informed that her baby was in a breech position.[39] A hospital obstetrician was strongly against the mother attempting a home vaginal birth and informed the mother orally and in writing that a caesarean section was highly recommended.[40] However, the mother was adamant she wanted a home birth. When the child was born she was not breathing, had no heartbeat and her umbilical cord was flat and blue.[41] Three midwives tried unsuccessfully to resuscitate the child. A hospital specialist who was called did manage to get a heartbeat, but it was too late and the child was taken off life support as early death or severe handicap were unavoidable.[42] The coroner said it was not possible to say whether the baby would have survived if the birth had taken place in a hospital, but the immediate availability of emergency care would have greatly reduced the possibility of death.[43]

The medical specialist who had tried to save the child complained to the New Zealand Nursing Council and the New Zealand College of Midwifery Standards Review Committee, saying that the interests of the baby should override the interests of the mother, such as the mother's preferences and desired place of delivery.[44] The two professional bodies found no case to answer.[45] The coroner was satisfied that the mother had made an informed choice to have a home birth, even though the midwives had done nothing to discourage the mother from having a home birth.[46] The midwives believed they could manage the mother's breech birth at home, which in fact they were not able to do.[47] The coroner recommended that the mother should not have a right to put the child at risk, and asked for the Code of Consumers' Rights to be amended to reflect this.[48] This has not happened. The hospital was asked to give women having breech babies more choices.[49] The New Zealand College of Midwives was asked by the coroner to give guidelines to midwives where there was a potential conflict between the mother's choice of birth and the baby's safety.[50]

The lack of trust between the healthcare professionals who are crucial for the birth of children has put patients in an intolerable dilemma; a dilemma that unnecessarily costs the lives of children. The sadness of it all is that both professions are dedicated to safe, healthy births, but the lack of trust and respect for each other gets in the way.

Leah Haines cites the example of a forum on natural birth where two senior midwives 'told the audience that they resorted to "deception" and "subterfuge" so obstetricians would not intervene in births that the doctors would likely think too risky, but which the midwives believed the mothers would be able to manage naturally'.[51] The most frightening aspect of a saga such as this is that once battle lines are drawn, each profession tends to bring out the worst in the other. A senior clinician who was interviewed found large discrepancies in rates of caesarean sections depending on which obstetrician was working that day.[52] Some obstetricians, for example, regularly performed twice as many caesareans as others.[53]

Once trust breaks down, it is likely to become a self-fulfilling prophecy. Everything the other profession does is seen through the lenses of distrust, which means that the worst possible interpretation is given, the most negative view of the other's motivation is taken. Behaviour becomes more entrenched, which may explain why there are higher rates of caesarean deliveries by some specialists, who may be asserting their dominance in relation to the midwives in the hospital.

Robin Youngson, an anaesthetist who was the clinical director at Waitakere Hospital, decided to break the deadlock at his hospital.[54] The pattern of behaviour that Youngson observed was that the midwives, with their primary focus on natural childbirth, believed that once an obstetrician became involved they would most likely prescribe a caesarean section. To avoid this, the midwives kept the obstetricians out of the picture unless there was a major crisis.[55] The obstetricians' response was to intervene and take mothers into surgery to prevent dangerous situations arising.[56] Every time this happened, the midwives saw it as removing control and power from the mother, and the medical specialists saw it as irresponsible midwives who put natural vaginal delivery above everything else, including the safety of the woman involved.[57] Such a climate makes it impossible for prospective mothers to make informed choices as to what is best for them.

Without trust between the professions of midwifery and obstetrics, concepts such as informed consent are meaningless. The information becomes distorted by the desire of each profession to portray itself more significantly than is necessary. The consent is not based on the range of birth options available and the risks and benefits of each. Informed consent becomes impossible when each profession sees itself as the only one providing benefits, while all the risks lie with the other profession. There will always be potential for bias towards one's own profession when information is given to patients, but this situation had gone well beyond potential bias to one where each profession could see no good at all in what the other profession had to offer pregnant women. Each thought they were superior, with no respect for the other.

The method used to break the downward spiral of distrust at Waitakere Hospital was to have what was called a 'Big Day Out'.[58] Role play was used to change the way the groups of healthcare professionals had been seeing one another.[59] According to an article about the event, a midwife who played the role of an obstetrician said at the end that she had 'never before realised that obstetricians cared about mothers and babies as she did'.[60] Which goes to show how deeply ingrained each profession's perceptions were about the other profession. Midwives' views may previously have been that the obstetricians did not care about the health and wellbeing of mothers and children, and that they only cared about their desire to carry out caesarean operations. Monthly, multidisciplinary maternity forums were carried out as a follow-up to reaffirm the changing patterns of perception.[61]

A measure of the success of the 'Big Day Out' was that the average caesarean rate at Waitakere Hospital fell from 27 per cent to 15 per cent.[62] However, the 'Big Day Out' approach did not have the same degree of success at other hospitals.[63] Dr Youngson put the success at Waitakere Hospital down to the quality of the interpersonal relationships between the professions, rather than any guidelines put out by the healthcare system.[64] For there to be good quality interpersonal relationships, there must be trust. Each profession must see themselves as equals in the quest to achieve safe and healthy childbirth. There will be disagreements as to what is best in some situations, but if each profession can act with goodwill and respect towards the other profession, difficulties are more likely to be worked out for the benefit of the patient.

The Ministry of Health published the 'Review of the Quality, Safety and Management of Maternity Services in the Wellington Area' (the Maternity Review) in October 2008.[65] The Ministry of Health commissioned the Maternity Review in 2008 after the death of a baby during a delivery. It found that both the New Zealand College of Midwives and the Royal Australian and New Zealand College of Obstetricians and Gynaecologists have focused on the provision of excellent maternity care in isolation from one another. No attempt had been made to develop joint standards for maternal care. The review team found it 'both significant and alarming to note that neither college's website specifies as a key role the need to work in a collaborative and supportive professional relationship with the other. Both colleges identify the need to work closely with women, but not with each other'.[66] A 'lack of respect, collegiality and collaboration between the obstetric and midwifery colleges', had led to 'some very poor relationships between individual midwives and obstetricians'.[67] The review team recommended greater collaboration between the professions to ensure 'seamless teamwork in the provision of maternity services to women and their babies',[68] and to jointly develop 'evidence-based standards for maternity care to which all relevant health professional groups subscribe'.[69] A proposal put forward by the review team to address the 'fundamental differences' between obstetricians and midwives to normal labour was to provide trainee doctors with the opportunity to observe midwifery practice.[70] From January 2011 it is recommended that 'obstetric registrar training include attachment to the practice of a self-employed LMC midwife or community-based team midwife in a primary or community setting, and involvement in births in this setting'.[71]

A major issue examined in the Maternity Review was the Primary Maternity Services Notice 2007 pursuant to section 88 of the New Zealand Public Health and Disability Act 2000.[72] The Maternity Notice provides for self-employed midwives to use public hospital facilities when their clients need or choose to give birth in a hospital.[73] This has led to the potential for different standards of care to apply within a hospital, depending on whether the practitioner is self-employed or works within the hospital. This should not happen if there are core principles of what best practice is. Forging working relationships between and across disciplines becomes much more difficult if healthcare professionals work in isolation and come in and out of hospitals without building working relationships with other healthcare professionals in the hospital. The Maternity Review team commented that 'safe and high-quality maternity services require excellent working relationships between all practitioners across the continuum of care'.[74] Excellent working relationships can only happen if the healthcare professionals involved in maternity care trust each other. This means equalising power, understanding what the other does and working together for the good of pregnant mothers. Surely patients have a right to this at the very least.

Breakdown of trust between healthcare professionals and patients and their families

Healthcare professionals have knowledge of medical matters that patients generally do not. Knowledge superiority can lead to inequality in the relationship between patients and healthcare professionals. Patients tend to know more about themselves in terms of how they are feeling and what has been happening to them over a period of time. Family members of patients who live with and observe the patient, over a long period of time, are also likely to know what has been happening to a patient. Respecting the knowledge that each has, and sharing that information, is most likely to lead to a good outcome for patients. Trust is the key to the relationship – the mindset that makes the effort to see that the other has equal power to you. Without equality between healthcare professionals, they erect barriers between each other, and the consequences are dire for the patients involved. Two highly publicised cases in New Zealand that involved children with cancer will be used to illustrate what happens when trust between healthcare professionals, patients and their families breaks down.

Liam Williams-Holloway

Liam Williams-Holloway, a 4-year-old boy, was diagnosed with a large neuroblastoma (tumour) on his jaw.[75] The oncologist gave Liam, at most, a 50 per cent chance of total recovery if the best available medical treatment was used.[76] Liam's parents agreed to go ahead with the chemotherapy treatment and Liam completed two sessions.[77] Liam's parents then told the oncologist that they wanted to look into alternative treatments because they were concerned about the side effects of the drug treatment on Liam, such as nosebleeds, nausea and vomiting.[78] The oncologist told the parents that if they wanted to use alternative treatment they should still continue with the chemotherapy. A 3-week break from the drug treatment was agreed to between the oncologist and the parents and then the chemotherapy would resume.[79] The reason for this was to ensure that the neuroblastoma did not 'recover' sufficiently to become resistant to the chemotherapy.[80] The parents had been doing their own research. Their view was that if the chemotherapy were resumed it would make Liam sick again, weaken his immune system and reduce the likelihood of the alternative treatment succeeding. After the two sessions of drug treatment, the tumour had reduced in size and this was put down to the alternative treatment by the parents. The alternative treatment consisted of 'quantum-boosting vibration therapy, painful body therapy and a special organic diet'.[81]

When the time came to resume the chemotherapy treatment, Liam's parents did not return with him, and instead took him into hiding.[82] Healthcare Otago, on behalf of Liam's oncologist, applied to the Family Court for Liam to be placed under the control of the court so that the court could then direct that the drug treatment be continued. The court made an order for Liam to be placed in the custody of the Children, Young Persons and Their Families Services with provisions for treatment to be resumed.[83]

Liam and his parents remained in hiding. New Zealand is not a big country but, after 4 months, Liam and his parents still could not be found. Public support kept them in hiding. The media fuelled public support for the parents.[84] The parents were interviewed in a national television programme called 'Holmes', as was Liam.[85] The healthcare professionals were portrayed as forcing the parents to take their child in for treatment they disagreed with. Healthcare Otago ultimately decided that the only option was to have the court order lifted so that the parents no longer had to be on the run from the law. The alternative therapist claimed they had cured Liam but sadly his tumour became larger. His parents then went to Mexico and Germany for him to have alternative treatments, surgery and chemotherapy. Liam died aged 5½ in Mexico in October 2000 because 'his tumour had progressed too far'.[86]

A survey of attitudes to parent/doctor conflicts over treatment for children carried out by Associate Professor Charlotte Paul of the Department of Preventative and Social Medicine at the Dunedin School of Medicine, University of Otago, Dunedin, New Zealand and four trainee interns found that there was strong support for seeking treatment orders from the courts in the child's best interests.[87] The members of the group surveyed were all academic staff at the University of Otago, both academic medical practitioners and non-health sciences academic staff. Seventy-seven per cent of those who responded to Liam's situation agreed with the doctor seeking a treatment order.[88] There was a major gender difference in the responses: 85 per cent of men agreed that a court application was the right way to go, with only 58 per cent of women agreeing with this.[89] A major reason for supporting court intervention was the child's best interests, particularly in what was seen as a life-and-death situation. Some of the responses to the survey went as far as saying there was an 'obligation' on doctors to intervene where the child is a young minor.[90] Those who supported intervention were of the view that the best evidence available showed that the best and highest chance for a cure was to use the conventional method of chemotherapy.[91] The success rate of at least 50 per cent was seen to outweigh the side effects for the child and override the parents' interests.[92] Alternative treatments were not seen as having any evidence base to support them. The members of this group were strongly of the view that 'specialists know what the best options are for a given patient, and this knowledge must be respected'.[93]

Those who opposed the court action took the view that such decisions are the 'responsibility of the parent' because they are the ones who have to 'live with the result of the decision'.[94] They also felt that a 50 per cent chance of a cure did not warrant court action and the side effects of chemotherapy.[95] Unlike those who were in favour of the court action and who thought the doctors had an obligation to intervene, this group thought it was 'arrogant' to override the parents' choices.[96] Ultimately, those opposed to court action thought that it was too aggressive, too destructive and that it destroyed the trust between parents and doctor.[97] Many of the (predominately female) participants in the study, who opposed court intervention – particularly the medically qualified women who would have some inside knowledge of medical behaviour – believed that further efforts should have been made to improve communication.[98] Charlotte Paul and her co-authors asked whether it was possible that 'if doctors behave differently, or if medication procedures are developed, compulsion could be avoided entirely?'[99] Many of the respondents to the survey felt that families had not been adequately informed or their knowledge of science was lacking. One of the participants commented: 'How poorly we explain the science of medicine to the public.'[100]

For Liam's parents to make the choice they did to use alternative treatment methods, they must have lost some degree of confidence in and trust of the chemotherapy treatment. It is not possible to know whether this was because of the way such treatment was put to the parents. If it was put in a way that they did not feel they were treated as equals, the likelihood is that trust would begin to erode at that point. It may be that the doctors did all they could to explore the options and explain their likely consequences to the parents, but that the parents had made up their minds once they saw the side effects of the chemotherapy on Liam. The bottom line of the survey carried out by the researchers in the Department of Preventative and Social Medicine at the University of Otago was that the majority of the participants supported court intervention where all other options to resolve disagreement between the doctors and the parents have been explored. There is no evidence of the outcome of treatment orders in New Zealand. The researchers suggest that there is 'anecdotal evidence that they often fail to achieve their desired outcomes'.[101] In order for trust between healthcare professionals and the families of sick children to flourish, these families need to know the options and likely outcomes in a realistic and non-pressurised manner.

Tovia Laufau

Soon after the Liam Williams-Holloway case was in the media, but before Liam passed away, a 13-year-old Samoan boy, Tovia Laufau, was diagnosed with osteosarcoma, a form of bone cancer in his knee.[102] Initially, Tovia complained of a sore leg and the mother took him to the family doctor. The diagnosis was an infection and antibiotics were prescribed.[103] Eight months later the left knee was still sore and Tovia was walking with a limp, which his parents thought was due to a rugby injury.[104] After five more visits to the doctor and a locum, there was no improvement to the knee. For all these visits, Tovia's mother took time off work to be with her son.[105] Tovia was then referred to a specialist who sent him to hospital for tests. For the 10 days he was in hospital being tested, Tovia's mother slept by his bed.[106] Scans showed a growth at the lower end of the thigh bone. A biopsy revealed osteosarcoma, a form of bone cancer, which had spread into tissues and muscles in the thigh bone. The medical diagnosis was that Tovia would die if he did not have surgery and chemotherapy.[107] The oncologist who made the initial diagnosis said that he told the family 'this tumour left untreated was fatal and could spread through the rest of Tovia's body and kill him'.[108] There were indications that the cancer had already spread to Tovia's lungs.[109] Tovia's mother said that her son was crying and frightened throughout the tests in the hospital.[110]

At the time the cancer was diagnosed, the oncologist at the hospital told the child's parents, Mr and Mrs Laufau, that with chemotherapy and surgery Tovia had a 60–70 per cent chance of making a full recovery.[111] Without treatment, the teenager would die. The parents said they would talk to their family before making a decision as to what to do and that they would return to the hospital with their decision the next day. The parents never returned to the hospital and never sought any further medical intervention.[112] They were approached by their GP, a Samoan social worker and a Samoan support worker, who visited the parents at their home and at their church.[113] The parents said that their son did not want treatment and they chose to put their faith in the power of prayer and in God, believing that was the best way for Tovia to be cured.

Six months later, Tovia died when the cancer spread to his lungs.[114] At the post-mortem, the tumour was found to weigh 15 kilograms.[115] Mr and Mrs Laufau were charged with manslaughter and failing to provide the necessities of life.[116] At the trial, Tovia's mother gave evidence that her son was so determined to avoid going to hospital for treatment for his cancer that he twice tried to jump from a moving car.[117] She also gave evidence that when Tovia learnt of the cancer he became very afraid and told his parents, 'Mum and Dad, if you ever take me back to hospital, I will never, ever, ever forgive you . . . If you take me to the hospital I will die straight away.'[118] The parents said that on many occasions they had tried to persuade him to go to hospital but he refused.

The community supported Mr and Mrs Laufau. The principal of Tamaki College, the school Tovia attended, said he knew the parents well and had 'tremendous respect' for them and the children they had raised.[119] He described the parents as 'very very religious' and said:

> If there was a concern that they did not seek enough medical help it would purely have been (because of) an absolute conviction that God was looking after them. You really need to understand the belief and sense of belief in that family . . . to really appreciate the situation . . . they believed God had chosen to take Tovia and that was right.[120]

The school principal went on to say that he believed the parents would be very confused as to why the police would be investigating them after Tovia had passed away.[121] According to the principal, at Tovia's funeral Mrs Laufau said that Tovia's father and sister were out when Tovia passed away.[122] Before he died, Tovia said to his mother, 'Mum, I just can't wait for Dad and Lydia – I've got to say goodbye, I'm too tired, I need to go now.'[123] Tovia's mother 'had an absolute conviction that God's angels had come down and taken him'.[124]

Dr Peter Watson was called as a defence witness at the parents' trial for manslaughter and failing to provide the necessities of life for Tovia. Dr Watson is a specialist in adolescent health from the Centre for Youth Health in South Auckland, the area where the Laufau family lived. In his evidence, Dr Watson placed the responsibility for Tovia's death solely on the healthcare system and hospital. Dr Watson said:

> This young man and other young people before him and in the future, I believe have and will suffer – not only suffer but also die – from the failure of the health system to recognise the unique needs of young people in our hospitals and provide appropriate services for them . . . It is also a tragedy for this family, and I would hope no other family ever has to be put through this experience when there is such an evident failure of the health system.[125]

Dr Watson said 'the medical world was full of jargon' and that 'it was critical for families to understand exactly what was being said at stressful times when bad news about complex issues was being given, especially when it was in a foreign language and in a "foreign" environment'.[126] Dr Watson said the healthcare system had a 'moral, ethical and legal duty to provide care' and that if the healthcare professionals failed to gain the trust and agreement of the family, they had an obligation to go 'farther afield and call in help to get them on-side' and ensure the family and the young boy understood what was happening.[127]

Tovia had become terrified of going back to the hospital. He had told his uncle that 'if he went to hospital his leg would be cut off and he would still die'.[128] This is a terrifying scenario for anyone to face, let alone a 13-year-old who would not have understood that the medical professionals were being brutally honest when they said that, even if his leg was removed, the cancer might still have spread to other parts of his body. At the trial, Tovia's mother gave evidence that her son thought he would die 'straight away' if he went back to the hospital.[129] Mrs Laufau also gave evidence that she feared her son might commit suicide if he was taken back to the hospital.[130] The parents believed their son was mature enough to make his own decision about his future health.[131]

Looked at from the family's point of view, the fact they never returned to hospital was inevitable. They had dealt with numerous medical personnel. They had visited two hospitals. Death had been talked about in both hospitals. All that the family, and in particular Tovia, could see was that the hospital was associated with the real possibility of him dying. Tovia and the family had lost trust in the hospital's healthcare professionals to improve his situation. They went back to what they understood best, the power of prayer.

It was clear that Tovia did not fully understand what could happen to him and neither did his parents. Whatever communication had been given to Tovia and his family had not been comprehended. Trust between the healthcare professionals, Tovia and his family had not been built: without it, the family did not want to come back and talk further. The healthcare professionals could see the picture clearly and no doubt they did what they believed was necessary to convey this to Tovia and his family. The different worlds both sides came from meant that establishing trust required more than simply explaining what the options were and what the likely consequences of each would be. For the family, this would be the first time they had faced such a huge decision for their son. It is likely to be the first time they had to discuss such an issue with healthcare professionals. Everything about the process would have been alien to them. On top of that is the stress of having a child with a tumour on his leg. That alone, without taking into account the fact there were language barriers for the family, would have made it difficult for Tovia and his family to fully understand what was happening.

Dr Jerome Groopman, a medical doctor and Professor of Medicine at Harvard, describes how he had undergone tests to diagnose pain and swelling in his right hand.[132] He underwent a bone scan. The radiologist saw some spots over his ribs.[133] The surgeon called Dr Groopman that evening and said 'there was no rush to operate on [his] hand because the spots on the scan looked like metastatic cancer in [his] ribs'.[134] Dr Groopman says he immediately felt pains in his chest and his ribs began to hurt.[135]

Dr Groopman is an oncologist who says that, if he were thinking rationally, he would have known that if his bones were riddled with tumours it would be unlikely there would have been no symptoms. But the news changed him from a doctor into a patient. He says 'my mind froze' and that he was 'overcome by fear' despite all his training and experience.[136] The pain in his chest felt very real. After further X-rays, it was found that his ribs were normal and that there were no spots. Dr Groopman describes the lessons he learnt from this episode thus:

> I learned two lessons from this episode. First, after shocking news was delivered in a blunt and absolute way, I needed someone to guide me, to provide balance, to raise doubt, to highlight uncertainty – to think for me and with me – because even though in another setting I would intellectually consider that the spots might be artifacts, I couldn't grasp it viscerally. Second, I experienced the power of the mind over the body, of psychosomatic symptoms.[137]

How could Tovia and his family even begin to understand the situation when a healthcare professional struggles once the news is personal to him? In order to begin to equalise power with the Laufau family, and therefore establish trust, the healthcare professionals needed to understand how frightening and emotionally distressing the news about the tumour on Tovia's leg would be. It was not simply a matter of informing the family that the leg would need to be removed, then discussing the ongoing treatment and what the chances of success were. It was a matter of understanding the shock and terror that the news created for the Laufau family. It is no wonder they retreated and did not want to come back. It is no wonder that the healing power of prayer was much more attractive to them than the news they were faced with by the doctors. The family desperately needed wider support at the time the diagnosis was being explained to them. Healthcare professionals need training about how young adolescents and their families are likely to receive such information. There is a human aspect to establishing trust that cannot be circumvented, no matter how clearly and fully information is explained to patients and their families. Onora O'Neill is right when she says that, without trust, concepts such as informed consent are meaningless.[138] As O'Neill says in the preface to her book *Autonomy and Trust in Bioethics*:

> Autonomy has been a leading idea in philosophical writing on bioethics; trust has been marginal ... Autonomy is usually identified with individual independence, and sometimes leads to ethically dubious or disastrous action. Its ethical credentials are not self-evident. Trust is surely

more important, and particularly so for any ethically adequate practice of medicine, science and biotechnology.[139]

The Laufau family were left with their own autonomy to make the decision, largely because they were not able to trust what they were being told by the healthcare professionals. If the Laufau family had been able to trust the healthcare professionals and what they were saying, the outcome for Tovia may have been different.

The hospital admitted that they had gone to court in the past to enforce treatment orders in such cases, but because of the bad publicity after the Liam Williams-Holloway case, in which healthcare professionals were criticised, they decided not to take this path.[140] The hospital staff also cited another case involving a 6-year-old Cook Island boy to justify their actions.[141] The boy was to have radiotherapy after removal of a brain tumour. His parents fled home with the child before the hospital's guardianship application was heard.[142] The child was returned when it was too late to save his life.[143] The hospital believed this showed the risk of applying to the court, in that it caused the parents to panic and take the child away. If the hospital had built a trusting relationship with the parents, there would have been no need to apply to the court.

Seventy per cent of the medical and academic staff at Otago University surveyed by Paul and her colleagues disagreed with the hospital's decision about the Laufau family.[144] The respondents believed the doctors had failed in their duty of care to Tovia. At the very least, if treatment was refused, there should have been every effort to provide palliative care. It was thought that a 13-year-old had the potential to understand the treatment. There was some gender difference in the response: 61 per cent of the female respondents and 76 per cent of the male respondents thought that the hospital staff should have sought a treatment order for Tovia.[145]

The outcome of the criminal trial was that Mr and Mrs Laufau were found not guilty of manslaughter, but guilty of failing to provide the necessities of life.[146] The jury rejected their defence that Tovia was mature enough to make his own decisions about medical treatment, and therefore there was a legal excuse not to bring him back in for treatment. It was explained to the jury by the trial judge, Potter J, that the fact that Tovia might have died from his cancer anyway, even with treatment, did not prevent the omission to get medical treatment from causing his death, if that failure to obtain medical treatment hastened Tovia's death.[147] Section 164 of the Crimes Act 1961 says that:

> Everyone who by any act or omission causes the death of another person kills that person, although the effect of the bodily injury caused to that person was merely to hasten his death while labouring under some disorder or disease arising from some other cause.[148]

In sentencing Mr and Mrs Laufau for failing to provide the necessities of life for Tovia, namely failing to take him into the hospital for treatment, Potter J said that:

> they are caring, conscientious parents who love their children dearly and whose every effort has been devoted to ensure that their children are brought up as members of a close-knit, caring family, and responsible members of the community, and that they are given the opportunity to take advantage of the education available to them and to achieve each of them, his or her own potential.[149]

Potter J also said:

> The duty the law imposes on parents and caregivers is greater and stronger than the wishes of their children, no matter how sincerely and strongly they might be expressed, and no matter how strong may be the wish or will of the parents to accede to the child's bidding.[150]

Potter J distinguished the right of an adult person with full mental faculties to exercise a right not to undergo medical treatment from the legal duty and responsibility of parents to ensure their child has medical treatment necessary to protect the child's life.[151] The difficulty for Mr and Mrs Laufau was that they believed in the power of prayer. They did not want their son to die; they probably did not fully understand the implications of the decision they made to support their son in his strong desire not to go back to hospital. Potter J described Mr and Mrs Laufau as 'responsible parents and citizens'.[152] It is harsh to find that they have been convicted of a criminal offence. They were ultimately sentenced to 15 months' imprisonment suspended for 15 months, which meant that as long as they behaved well they would not spend any time in prison.[153] They were subject to supervision for 15 months to enable them to have the assistance of professional help.

To subject the healthcare professionals, who should have gone further in seeking treatment for Tovia, to criminal prosecution will not help similar situations in the future. It is also unlikely that such a prosecution would succeed. There needs to be a 'major departure from the standard of care expected' of a reasonable healthcare professional in the circumstances.[154] As the survey shows, not all healthcare professionals believe it is appropriate to apply for a treatment order in circumstances such as this case.[155] The doctors were not 'in charge' of Tovia', his parents were. If the doctors were in charge of him, they would have had a duty to provide the necessities of life.[156] The doctors would have been in charge of Tovia if the parents had placed him in their care in the hospital.

The threat of criminal prosecution in such cases is likely to lead to more applications for treatment orders in circumstances where it would be preferable to work more closely with the parents. The best solution to what happened to Tovia is for healthcare professionals to build trust with families where there are children who need treatment. This can only be done by treating those families as equals, understanding how those families see the world, listening to their concerns and exploring options in a way the family will understand. This will take time, patience and empathy but it will be worth it if it means families and healthcare professionals can work together to save young lives in the future.

Notes

1 Right 4(5) of the Code of Health and Disability Services Consumers' Rights as prescribed by the Health and Disability Commissioner (Code of Health and Disability Services Consumers' Rights) Regulations 1996.

2 Haines, L, 'Another Unfortunate Experiment', *New Zealand Listener* 217, 2009, p 14.

3 Ibid, p 15.

4 Health and Disability Commissioner, *Midwife, Mrs B: A Rural Maternity Hospital*, Opinion 07HDC16053, 10 June 2008, p 12.

5 The Nurses Amendment Act 1990 changed the provisions of maternity services in New Zealand from being primarily the domain of medical practitioners to increasingly the domain of midwives. Midwives are now able to offer the full range of antenatal, labour, birth and postnatal services without the supervision of a doctor.

6 Op. cit., Haines, p 15.

7 The Royal Australian and New Zealand College of Obstetricians and Gynaecologists, *Maternity Services Review Submission*, 31 October 2008, p 100.

8 Ibid, p 101.

9 Op. cit., Haines, p 16.

10 The phrase came from the title of an article that exposed what had been happening at National Women's Hospital. See Coney, S and Bunkle, P, 'An "Unfortunate Experiment" at National Women's', *Metro*, June 1987. This ultimately led to Cartwright, S, *The Report of the Cervical Cancer Inquiry 1988*, Auckland: Government Printing Office, 1988.

11 Crawford, B *et al*, *Review of the Quality, Safety and Management of Maternity Services in the Wellington Area*, Ministry of Health, 2008, p 18.

12 Ibid.

13 Ibid, p 41.

14 Ibid, p 42.

15 Health and Disability Commissioner, *Midwife, Ms B; Midwife, Ms C*, Case 04HDC05503, 28 November 2006, p 2.

16 Ibid.

17 Ibid.

18 Ibid, pp 8–9.

19 *R v Crawshaw*, HC Dunedin CRI-2005-012-001860, 6 March 2006, 'Notes of Evidence Taken Before the Honourable Justice Panckhurst and a Jury of Twelve', p 24.

20 Ibid.

21 Ibid, p 25.

22 Ibid, p 48.

23 Ibid, p 70.

24 Ibid.
25 Ibid.
26 Ibid, p 86.
27 Ibid.
28 Ibid, p 88.
29 Ibid, p 116.
30 Ibid, p 117.
31 Ibid, p 129.
32 Ibid, p 193.
33 Ibid, p 327.
34 Op. cit., *Midwife, Ms B; Midwife, Ms C*, p 9.
35 Op. cit., *R v Crawshaw*, p 233.
36 Op. cit., *Midwife, Mrs B: A Rural Maternity Hospital*, p 9.
37 Ibid, p 8.
38 *An Inquest into the Death of Isabell Grace Riddell*, Coroners Court Hamilton 970506, 24 April 1997, p 6.
39 Ibid, p 2.
40 Ibid, p 2.
41 Ibid.
42 Ibid, p 3.
43 Ibid, p 5.
44 Ibid.
45 Ibid, p 4.
46 Ibid, p 5.
47 Ibid.
48 Ibid, p 6.
49 Ibid.
50 Ibid.
51 Op. cit., Haines, p 18.
52 Ibid, pp 18–19.
53 Ibid.
54 Ibid, p 19.
55 Ibid.
56 Ibid.
57 Ibid.
58 Youngson, R, Wimbrow, T and Stacey, T, 'A Crisis in Maternity Services: The Courage to be Wrong', *Quality and Safety in Health Care* 12, 2003, p 398.
59 Ibid, pp 398–399.
60 Ibid, p 399.
61 Ibid.
62 Ibid, pp 398, 400.
63 The Hutt Valley Hospital and the Otago District Health Board employed a similar approach to some success, but neither place achieved the results seen at Waitakere Hospital. Haines, op. cit., p 19.
64 Op. cit., Haines, p 19.
65 The members of the review team were Barbara Crawford (Chairperson) – Manager Quality and Risk, Waikato District Health Board; Siniua Lilo – National Manager Customer Relations, ANZ Bank; Professor Peter Stone – Head of Department of Obstetrics and Gynaecology, Faculty of Medical and Health Sciences, University of Auckland; and Ann Yates – Midwifery Leader, Auckland District Health Board. Crawford *et al*, op. cit., p. 6.
66 Ibid, p 41.
67 Ibid, p 16.

68 Ibid, p 42.
69 Ibid, p 9.
70 Ibid, p 50.
71 Ibid.
72 Ibid, pp 31–37.
73 Ibid, p 31.
74 Ibid, p 36.
75 Paul, C *et al*, 'A Survey of Attitudes to Parent-Doctor Conflicts Over Treatment for Children', *The New Zealand Medical Journal* 114, 2001, p 550.
76 Ibid.
77 Ibid.
78 Ibid.
79 Ibid.
80 Ibid.
81 Ibid.
82 Ibid.
83 Ibid.
84 Ansley, B, 'Mind That Child', *New Zealand Listener* 3080, 1999, p 18.
85 Ibid.
86 Op. cit., Paul *et al*, p 550.
87 Ibid. The trainee interns involved were Sharon Brandon, Deborah Clarke, Angela George and Janice Jensen.
88 Ibid. Eighty-two respondents out of a total of 107 agreed with Liam Williams-Holloway's doctor taking court action.
89 Ibid.
90 Ibid.
91 Ibid.
92 Ibid.
93 Ibid.
94 Ibid.
95 Ibid.
96 Ibid.
97 Ibid.
98 Ibid, p 552.
99 Ibid.
100 Ibid.
101 Ibid.
102 *R v Laufau* [2001] NZLJ 82, at [2].
103 Larkin, N, 'Parents' Agony Over Son They Loved to Death', *New Zealand Herald*, 25 August 2000.
104 Ibid.
105 Ibid.
106 Ibid.
107 Ibid.
108 Ibid.
109 Ibid.
110 Ibid.
111 Op. cit., *R v Laufau*, at [2].
112 Ibid.
113 Ibid.
114 Op. cit., Paul *et al*, p 550.
115 Ibid.
116 Under ss 152 and 171 of the Crimes Act 1961.

117 'Cancer-Stricken Boy Tried to Jump From Car: Mother', *New Zealand Herald*, 22 August 2000.
118 Ibid.
119 Wall, T, 'Parents Put Boy's Cancer into Hands of God', *New Zealand Herald*, 12 October 1999.
120 Ibid.
121 Ibid.
122 Ibid.
123 Ibid.
124 Ibid.
125 Op. cit., Larkin.
126 'Specialist Blasts System Failures in Cancer Boy Case', *New Zealand Herald*, 23 August 2000.
127 Ibid.
128 Ibid.
129 Op. cit., 'Cancer-Stricken Boy Tried to Jump From Car: Mother'.
130 Op. cit., Larkin.
131 Ibid.
132 Groopman, J, *How Doctors Think*, Melbourne: Scribe Publications, 2007, p 265.
133 Ibid.
134 Ibid.
135 Ibid, p 266.
136 Ibid.
137 Ibid.
138 O'Neill, O, *Autonomy and Trust in Bioethics*, Cambridge: Cambridge University Press, 2002.
139 Ibid, p ix.
140 Wall, T, 'Liam Case Worried Mangere Boy Carers', *New Zealand Herald*, 15 October 1999.
141 Johnston, M, 'Cancer Boy Dies After Lack of Care', *New Zealand Herald*, 25 August 2000.
142 Ibid.
143 Ibid.
144 Op. cit., Paul *et al*, p 551.
145 Ibid.
146 'Family Weep at Cancer Boy Verdict', *New Zealand Herald*, 24 August 2000.
147 Ibid.
148 Crimes Act 1961, s 164.
149 Op. cit., *R v Laufau*, at [4].
150 Ibid, at [15].
151 Ibid.
152 Ibid, at [16].
153 Ibid, at [19].
154 Crimes Act 1961, s 150A.
155 Op. cit., Paul *et al*, p 551.
156 Crimes Act 1961, s 151.

Chapter 6

Trust, emerging technologies and indigenous peoples

Advances in medical science provide new choices and dilemmas that can be frightening or bewildering. The first heart transplant and the first 'test-tube' baby raised concerns that we were meddling with nature and playing god.[1] Who and what can we trust in making such choices? Ethics and its modern sub-brand of bioethics have filled the vacuum and attempted to provide answers.[2]

According to James Flynn, 'Thrasymachus presents Plato with a dual challenge: if reason defined as the scientific method is the only road to knowledge, it discloses no ethical truth; and even if there were such a thing as true justice, it would be purely academic.'[3] In the real world, what orders society is politics, and the underlying value of politics is that 'might makes right'.[4] Academia has its own political world of power and hierarchy: 'Might is right' in the sense of dominant discourses being given the most airtime.[5] In an ideal society, Plato assumed that there would be some method that 'generates unity of opinion about the good'.[6] But once we have found that method, we have destroyed the very thing many of us treasure most – 'that we are wholly free, not only to choose for ourselves what we ought to do, but to decide for ourselves, individually and as a species, what we ought to be'.[7] As Flynn states of truth-tests:

> I believe that even if a particular truth-test were valid, even if it were to vindicate humane ideals, it would distort them in the process of vindicating them. It would strip humane ideals of their capacity to generate humane reasons for the goodness of acts. This is a necessary consequence of truth-tests: the fact that they elevate a nonpartisan criterion of right and wrong above humane ideals necessitates the downgrading of humane ideals.[8]

Autonomy is currently the dominant value in bioethical[9] and legal literature on genetics.[10] Autonomy begs the question of whose autonomy should be given priority in which situations? Autonomy as a value does not necessarily clash with trust. Trust requires the effort to equalise power with others, which is a way of recognising their individuality, their autonomy. Without trust, there is not much point in having autonomy. Such autonomy, without trust, could only exist in a world of 'might is right'. The outcome would be: my autonomy is more important than your autonomy. As O'Neill puts it, 'Individual autonomy is most readily expressed when we are least constrained by others and their expectations.'[11] By way of contrast, 'Trust is most readily placed in others whom we can rely on to take our interests into account, to fulfil their roles, to keep their parts in bargains.'[12] As O'Neill says in a nutshell, 'Trust belongs with relationships and (mutual) obligations; individual autonomy with rights and adversarial claims.'[13] The risk of making autonomy the Holy Grail is that this perspective endangers trust. As O'Neill states, 'If we are worried about loss of trust, we may wonder whether and why individual autonomy should now be so much admired.'[14]

This chapter will show the differences that can be achieved if trust is the central value when analysing the choices that new discoveries pose, with a particular emphasis on their impact on indigenous peoples who have been vulnerable to abuses of trust.

Havasupai Tribe v Arizona Board of Regents

The Havasupai tribe live in the Supai village at the bottom of the Grand Canyon in Arizona in the United States.[15] An anthropology professor at the Arizona State University, John Martin, began studying the Havasupai tribe in 1963[16] and built up a strong relationship with the people. Work was carried out in collaboration with the Havasupai tribe on education issues, community issues, community action and development programmes, and social and environmental studies. In 1989, a member of the Havasupai tribe asked Martin to do some research into what was seen as an 'epidemic' of diabetes among tribe members.[17] Martin hypothesised that the diabetes was related to genetics and diet. Arizona State University Genetics Professor Therese Markow agreed to undertake the research, which was called a 'diabetes-centred project'.[18] Markow wanted to add research into schizophrenia as part of the project. Martin told her the Havasupai tribe would not be interested in such an extension to the study, but did not totally rule out such a possibility.[19] Without discussing it with the Havasupai tribe, Markow successfully applied for a research grant to study schizophrenia among tribe members.[20]

Two hundred Havasupai people signed informed consent forms to give their blood for what they believed was research on diabetes within their tribe. The researchers concluded that diabetes was developing too quickly among tribal members for it to be relevant to genetics.[21] Markow published a paper in 1991 reporting that there was too little variation among the Havasupai people's genetics to 'conclude the incidence of the disease among them was genetics-related'.[22]

Unbeknown to the members of the Havasupai tribe, the researchers at Arizona State University and elsewhere, including the University of Arizona, continued to perform research and publish articles based on the blood samples taken from the tribe members.[23] Four doctrinal dissertations and a number of academic papers were published using evidence obtained from the blood samples.[24] The publications dealt with a variety of issues totally unrelated to the informed consent given, such as evolutionary genetics, 'schizophrenia, inbreeding and theories about ancient human population migrations from Asia to North America'.[25] Theories into ancient human population migrations from Asia were directly contrary to the Havasupai tribe's belief that they originated from the Grand Canyon.[26]

In 2002, Martin found out that non-diabetes research was continuing on the samples.[27] In 2003, the Havasupai tribe asked Arizona State University for information on what had happened to their samples.[28] Eventually, after the researchers were banned from the Havasupai Reservation, the University commissioned an agreement with the Havasupai tribe for an independent report to look into:

> the circumstances surrounding the collection of blood samples and other research data from members of the Havasupai Tribe and any and all subsequent uses of the sample or their derivatives and other research data for research or other purposes.[29]

Unsuccessful settlement meetings followed before the matter proceeded to trial. The Havasupai tribe claimed $50 million from the university alleging breach of fiduciary duty, lack of informed consent, fraud, misrepresentation, fraudulent concealment, intentional infliction of emotional distress, conversion, violation of civil rights, negligence and gross negligence.[30]

The university, after spending $1.7 million fighting the claims in court, eventually settled with the tribe for $700,000 and issued a public apology.[31] The university agreed to return the blood samples they still had, collaborate with the Havasupai tribe on matters such as health, education and economic development, and create a scholarship programme for tribal members.[32]

The breach of trust was deeply personal. The Havasupai tribe were upset that Markow and others had used their blood samples in a way that the Havasupai people had not consented too. The Havasupai tribe gave their blood samples to the researchers in an effort to understand the epidemic of diabetes they were experiencing. However, the researchers went on to use the tribe's blood samples to research schizophrenia, inbreeding and the ancestral origins of the Havasupai people. In interviews with *The New York Times*, members of the Havasupai tribe expressed deep feelings of betrayal, particularly by Arizona State University for putting their blood through genetic testing to link the origins of the Havasupai people to Asia. The Havasupai people had a long tradition of stories that linked their origins to the Grand

Canyon itself. As Rex Tilousi, a Havasupai tribe member, states, 'It hurts the elders who have been telling these stories to our grandchildren.'[33] This new information went to the very core of their being, without giving the Havasupai people any opportunity to say whether they wanted such an inquiry.

The Havasupai people were not against scientific research *per se*; rather, they felt betrayed because they did not give permission for their blood to be used for the later scientific research, which was offensive to their cultural beliefs. As Carletta Tilousi, a member of the Havasupai tribal council, said, 'I'm not against scientific research . . . I just want it to be done right. They used our blood for all these studies, people got degrees and grants, and they never asked our permission.'[34] As Hank Greely, Director of the Centre for Law and the Biosciences at Stanford University, states, this kind of behaviour 'sows distrust . . . And researchers cannot do their research unless people are willing to trust them'.[35] Mary Pember described the Havasupai case as 'an example of the paternalism that has dominated the relationship between academic researchers and tribes for generations'.[36] Dr Sonya Alalay, a member of the Anishinabe tribe and Assistant Professor of Anthropology at Indiana University, said: 'There continues to be a sense that Western ways of knowing and understanding are more important and therefore give researchers the right of way in understanding the world.'[37] When researches adopt this atti-tude, they do not try to equalise power and thereby they fail to build trust and become trustworthy. Such an attitude gives researchers a sense of entitlement, of might is right and of individual careers coming before a whole people's sense of wellbeing. The Arizona State University researchers had no sense of mutual obligation to the people who had given their blood samples for their research.

In a formal public apology to the tribe, Ernest Calderon, President of the Arizona Board of Regents, said: 'The Board of Regents has long wanted to remedy the wrong that was done. This solution is not simply the end of a dispute but is also the beginning of a partnership between the universities, ASU and the Tribe.'[38] Dr Daniel Wildcat of the Muscogee tribe, Professor of American Indian Studies at Haskell Indian Nations University, puts the university's apology in its context: 'They had no choice . . . but to settle if they expected to work with any Indian communities in the future.'[39]

The Guaymi patent claim

Type II of the rare human T-cell lymphotrophic viruses (HTLV) is known to be the causative agent of adult T-cell leukaemia and a neurological disease.[40] Infection with HTLV type II is common among the Guaymi of Panama as well as other American Indian peoples in North and South America.[41] A project carried out by the Centre for Disease Control of the United States Department of Health and Human Services and the National Institutes of Health, in collaboration with Panamanian scientists, was designed to look into why infection with HTLV led to cell leukaemia.[42] The President of the General Congress of the Guaymi people, Isidro Acosta, is quoted as saying:

> Doctors came to the communities of Pandilla in small groups and started to collect indigenous blood, pretending that the indigenous people were suffering from a mortal disease and that the blood study was necessary to investigate the malformation or type of disease they suffered. Participants were given a small pill to compensate for the loss of blood.[43]

It was discovered that one of three Guaymi women suffering from leukaemia had an unusual ability to resist the disease.[44] A patent application was filed by the United States National Institutes of Health for a T-cell line infected with HTLV-II developed from blood donated by the Guaymi people. The Centre for Disease Control of the United States Department of Health claimed that the purpose of the patented cell line was to make the line available to researchers.[45] The patent application was filed without any notification to the Guaymi woman who had the capacity to resist leukaemia, or to any other Guaymi people.[46] The Panamanian government and the collaborative researchers from that country were not told about the patent application until after it had been filed, 'first in the United States and later worldwide under the Patent Cooperative Treaty (an international agreement that makes it possible for a single patent application to be filed in several countries in which patent protection is desired)'.[47]

When the World Council of Indigenous Peoples and the General Congress of the Ngöbe-Buglé (Guaymi) found out about the patent application, and the circumstances in which it was obtained, they publicly condemned it.[48] Isidro Acosta, President of the General Congress of the Ngöbe-Buglé (Guaymi) wrote to both the United Nations Secretary of Commerce and the Patents and Trademarks Office to reject the patent application.[49] At the General Agreement on Tariffs and Trade Secretariat, Isidro Acosta said that to patent living cells was to patent private property and that it was 'against all Guaymi traditions and laws'.[50]

Ultimately, the patent application was withdrawn. The reason given was the high cost of pursing it.[51] Darrell Posy and Graham Dutfield suggest that, 'It seems more likely that the real reason the claim was abandoned was the international outcry.'[52]

The actions of the United States researchers show a belief that their endeavours are more important than the people from whom the blood samples were taken. Their right to try and solve the pathways of adult T-cell leukaemia was seen as more important than the sensitivities and beliefs of the people whose cells had made their research possible. There was no attempt to equalise power with the Guaymi people. They were simply seen as a means to an end for the US medical researchers. No thought was given to the dignity and equality of the indigenous people.

The Hagahai of Papua New Guinea

A blood sample from a member of the Hagahai people of Papua New Guinea was used to develop a cell line that was infected with a local variant of HTLV-I.[53] The purpose was to develop vaccines and diagnostic tools to screen and treat Melanesian people infected with the HTLV-I virus. The Hagahai people are a group of approximately 260 indigenous people in Papua New Guinea.[54] The United States National Institutes of Health filed a patent application for a cell line formed from a member of the Hagahai people's blood. In 1995, a United States patent was granted over the cell line 'in spite of objections from the Papua New Guinea government'.[55] In 1996, after extensive pressure from the indigenous people and the international community, the patent on the human cell line of the Hagahai indigenous person was withdrawn by the United States National Institutes of Health.[56] Alejandro Argumedo of the Canada-based Indigenous People's Biodiversity Network said, 'I hope this is the end of what is arguably the most offensive patent ever issued.'[57] Neth Dano, of the South East Asia Regional Institute for Community Education in the Philippines, pointed out the contradiction in the US government's responses to this particular patent. As Dano said:

> If, as the US State Department said, the Hagahai patent was 'for their benefit', why did the US not even bother to contact the Hagahai when it gave up the patent? Why does NIH blame a researcher in Papua New Guinea for the US Government's own patent? The Papua New Guinea Institute for Medical Research has said that it followed NIH's lead.[58]

Aroha Mead, of the Maori (the indigenous people of New Zealand) Congress, sums up the feelings of indigenous people after the Hagahai patent was withdrawn thus:

> While the US may have now disclaimed the Hagahai patent, a trail of trauma and mistrust has been left behind . . . The patent deeply affected indigenous peoples of the Pacific. It sent a message to Pacific communities that researchers cannot be trusted and it will take a long time to convince them otherwise. While the Hagahai patent is dropped, which unsuspecting community will it be tomorrow?[59]

The idea of trust features strongly in indigenous people's reaction to what happened with the Hagahai people. The indigenous Hagahai person from Papua New Guinea who donated his cells was not treated as an equal by the researcher or by the United States National Institutes of Health. The Hagahai person was a means to an end for creating a cell line that was then was quickly turned into the property of the United States National Institutes of Health by lodging the patent. The Hagahai indigenous person was not seen as an equal collaborator in the research, but was simply seen instead as a set of convenient cells that could be used for financial gain. The US government argued that it had the informed consent of the Hagahai people and the approval of the Papua New Guinea government for the patent but produced nothing to substantiate these claims.[60]

The Solomon Islands patent claims

A woman from the Solomon Islands, with a history of hepatitis contracted through a blood transfusion, and a man with an enlarged liver and spleen, provided cells which contained a local HTLV-I viral strain from which a T-cell line was developed and a patent lodged by the United States National Institutes of Health.[61] The claim was that the Solomon Islanders gave their informed consent to samples being taken.[62] Officials from the Solomon Islands were very concerned about the patent application and did not want the patent to be granted.[63] The Solomon Islands United Nations ambassador wrote a letter of protest to the United States Department of Commerce about the patent application. Former Department of Commerce Secretary Ron Brown stated in response:

> Under our laws, as well as those of many other countries, subject matter relating to human cells is patentable and there is no provision for considerations relating to the source of the cells that may be the subject of a patent application.[64]

Ultimately, the United States National Institutes of Health withdrew the patent application for the Solomon Islands cell line in 1994.[65] The reason for this withdrawal was not because of the protest by Solomon Islands officials, but rather 'because it appeared that the demand for commercial products that might be produced from this cell line was low'.[66]

So-called informed consent does not mean much if it is not fully understood and where those obtaining it have a wider financial motivation. Without trust, informed consent is an empty shell. All the cases cited here have as their common denominator the desire to discover new knowledge, which is not a bad thing. But they all have a lack of fully collaborating with and involving the people from whom the samples have been taken. Only part of the story has been shared with the indigenous people. The full implications of commercialising their cell lines and using them for other purposes were consistently kept in the background.

The 'warrior gene' story as a catalyst for building trust[67]

A headline, 'Warrior Gene Blamed for Maori Violence', was breaking news around the world in August 2006.[68] An Australian scientist, Dr Rod Lea, who was working in New Zealand, said that Maori men have a 'striking over-representation' of the monoamine oxidase gene that is 'strongly associated' with risk taking and aggressive behaviour – 'it definitely predisposes people to be more likely to be criminals'.[69] Dr Tony Merriman, a genetic scientist at the University of Otago, New Zealand, was of the view that Dr Rod Lea's claims did not stack up scientifically.[70] Dr Merriman, and his colleague, Dr Vicky Cameron, found longitudinal studies that showed the crucial fact was whether or not the person had been severely mistreated as a child, and that 'high' monoamine oxidase-A (MAO-A) alleles were protection against antisocial behaviour, even where there had been severe maltreatment.[71] Many Maori were rightfully upset by the findings, which appeared to say they had a gene that made them more likely to be criminals. With Maori making up a high proportion of those in prison in New Zealand, the 'warrior gene' headline furthered a stereotype that some sections of New Zealand society wanted to believe anyway.[72] The gap between the headline and the realities of the longitudinal studies potentially disempowered Maori people in New Zealand.

A major New Zealand study on the implications of the discovery and sequences of the human genome, *Genes, Society and the Future: Volume I*, found that there are a number of areas of criticism of genetic studies involving indigenous people.[73] These comprise the exclusion of indigenous people from the planning and design of such research; disregard of different cultural values about conditions; insufficient reporting to communities about research results; the potential for community stigmatisation as a result of badly managed publication of research results; arguments over who owns DNA; community perceptions of exploitation; and fears about the unauthorised research use of stored DNA and cell lines.[74] The balance of power between the indigenous communities and researchers is out of sync in all the case studies discussed in this chapter. *Genes, Society and the Future: Volume 1* recommends that test results should be reported back to the community and that, 'Genetic samples should be considered "on loan" to the researchers for the specific purposes for which consent was obtained.'[75] Some researchers will say that this gives too much power to the community. But if the researcher builds a good relationship with the community then, from that trust, the researcher is much more likely to carry out better research.[76]

Because Dr Rod Lea lived within the community he was carrying out his research on, and because he had set up a wide range of health benefits for their participation in his study, the Rakaipaaka people he was working with continued to trust him even after the 'warrior gene' headline burst into the media. The people could see the immediate health benefits they were gaining from their participation in the study. The study was wide ranging, looking at all aspects of the 3,000-strong community's wellbeing and encouraging healthy eating and habits. The release into the media of the 'warrior gene' idea sharpened the community's awareness of what was at stake when genetic research is done.

The community controlled the research project. The Maori tribe, known as Te Iwi o Rakaipaaka, entered into an agreement in 2005 with the Institute of Environmental Science and Research, a Crown Research Institute set up by the New Zealand government.[77] A comprehensive consultation and negotiation process was carried out over several months before the agreement was signed. Local people welcomed the genetics-based healthcare research. One member of the Rakaipaaka people said:

> I felt excited at the time; it was one way of getting health services coming to our people in Nuhaka, to start looking at the ways we need to make ourselves well, to address concerns of health that were taking our people beyond the veil before their time.[78]

The research agreement between the Institute of Environmental Science and Research and the Rakaipaaka people stated that 'the genetic information from this project cannot be used for secondary studies without the express permission of Ngati Rakaipaaka [the Rakaipaaka people]'.[79]

Participants in the study were provided with access to a general practitioner of medicine (GP), free health screening and healthcare planning. The Rakaipaaka people live in a rural area where there is a major shortage of healthcare services.[80] The purpose of the research is to identify the 'serious diseases and conditions common amongst the Rakaipaaka community, and analyse the potential for underlying genetic-based explanations for the conditions'.[81] The study investigated how the genetic explanations interact with lifestyle and environmental factors. Some of the Rakaipaaka people suffer from conditions such as cancer, diabetes and strokes at disproportionately higher rates than those of the standard population.[82]

If the research leads to the discovery of a particular genetic marker being able to be used in a new way to help predict future diseases, then the Rakaipaaka people themselves will take out the patent.[83] The research moves at a pace that the Rakaipaaka people are comfortable with. As a spokesman for the people said:

> We want to be a Maori organisation or Maori people that can say we've instigated this because we feel this is the way we want and we're going to do it the way we feel is more comfortable for us to do. For instance, instead of a non-Maori organisation that's going to drive this, it's going to be us. We're going to drive this in the way we want it to be driven. These are the benefits, only Maori can realise that they are the only ones who can be the architects of their own development to reach their full potential . . . This is one way we can show ourselves that we can do it. We're looking at sharing with other communities that this could happen to.[84]

The potential for the Rakaipaaka people to take out patent protection over genetic date collected from their members raised considerable ethical issues for them. In particular, questions were raised about the right of an Iwi (tribe) to take out a life patent on genetic markers that are not only common to Rakaipaaka, but are associated with the wider Polynesian population.[85] Most important for the members of the Iwi was that their whakapapa (their ancestral lineage) was not abused or commercialised by others.

There are strong reasons for not allowing gene patents. Generally, applicants who seek human gene patents argue they have isolated and purified a gene and produced something novel. The newness is 'a product whose noncoding regions have been eliminated, but which still performs the same function as a naturally-occurring gene'.[86] Some gene patents are claims to gene segments that occur in nature and exist in human bodies. For example, US Patent Number 5679135 claims the genetic sequence of the aspartoacylase gene and protein.[87] Lori Andrews and Jordan Paradise point out that the 'discovery of genes does not require the same commercial incentives as drug development'.[88] Drugs have been developed primarily with private funds, where investors expect a financial return on their investment, while public funds have been the primary source in genomic research.[89]

Andrews and Paradise point out that Myriad, the US genetics company that first patented BRCA1 (a gene associated with susceptibility to breast and ovarian cancer), 'used over five million dollars from a government agency when researching the patent and utilized sequence data from public databases'.[90] The result is the public pay twice – first for the research and then for the royalty costs charged to use the patented gene in a product.[91] Developing drugs requires expensive clinical trials to bring it into use. The discovery of a gene does not incur this cost, so there is less need for the financial recompense that patents bring.

Access to appropriate healthcare is compromised when exclusive licensing of a gene patent is permitted. As Andrews and Paradise point out, 'Various mutations in the same gene can cause a particular disease, but companies that do not let anyone else test for "their" gene make it more difficult for the discovery of other significant mutations in that gene.'[92] For example, in countries where the Alzheimer's and haemochromatosis genes were not patented, researchers discovered previously unknown mutations.[93] These new mutations meant that those who would not have been diagnosed by the original discovery and consequent genetics test could now be picked up.

Once a patent is granted over a gene, the patent holder controls the price and this makes it impossible for the equitable distribution of healthcare. Medical progress can be blocked. Andrews and Paradise use the example of a patent holder forbidding anyone from using the genetic sequence it has patented, even if the patent holder does not offer a diagnostic test using that sequence, to show the impact on future healthcare.[94] Andrews and Paradise also use the example of a pharmaceutical company that has filed for a patent on a genetic test to determine the effectiveness of its asthma drug, yet does not plan to develop the test or let anyone else develop it.[95]

Allowing patents over genes or gene sequences puts too much power in the hands of the discoverer, at the expense of public health. Researchers, if they want to be trusted by their communities, must equalise power and share their knowledge of discovering gene mutations for the good of everyone. The discovery, which is what science is all about, will enhance their scientific reputation; the sharing of their knowledge will enhance their trustworthiness and lead to more willingness by the public to work with the researchers in the future.

The Rakaipaaka research meets the guidelines developed by the New Zealand National Ethics Advisory Committee for developing a Maori framework for ethical review of health and disability research. The principles are based on the Treaty of Waitangi, a document signed by a large number of Maori chiefs and representatives of the British Crown in 1840 at Waitangi, in the far north of New Zealand. The document's true meaning is still contested.[96] It has been assumed to be the document that gave the British Crown authority to have 'sovereignty' in New Zealand. The key principles are:

1   Partnership – working with Iwi, Hapu, Whanau and Maori organisations to ensure Maori individual and collective rights are respected and protected.
2   Participation – involving Maori in the decisions, governance, management implementation and analysis of research, especially research involving Maori.
3   Protection – actually protecting Maori individual and collective rights, Maori data and Maori cultural values, norms, practices and language in the research project.

Dr Parry Guilford and his team of researchers from the Cancer Genetics Laboratory at the University of Otago, New Zealand are a model example of how the building of trust can lead to both positive outcomes for an indigenous community and also a scientific breakthrough that is most likely to benefit others.[97] An extended family of Maori people (the indigenous people of New Zealand) was plagued with stomach cancer.[98] Dr Guilford and his team hypothesised that there was likely to be a genetic marker for the cancer within the family group. The researchers spent a number of years building a relationship with the family, explaining the theory to them and the implications if a genetic marker was discovered for the stomach cancer. The researchers worked in collaboration with the family, building strong bonds of trust.

After 10 years, a specific genetic marker of the stomach cancer within this family was discovered.[99] Mutations in the E-cadherin gene were identified in family members who were highly susceptible to developing gastric cancer. One letter in a code of three billion letters was out of sequence.[100] The particular gene is central to cell adhesion and structure and is thought to support cell invasion. The gene is switched off in those who have the mutation. Dr Guilford found that 70 per cent of people with the mutation contracted the disease.[101] This meant that members of the family could be tested for this marker. The researchers developed a relatively simple blood test.[102] Of the 133 people from the extended family who were tested, 47 were found to have the mutated E-cadherin gene.[103] These people were then screened by a chrome-endoscopy technique, which uses coloured dyes to enhance the appearance of the cancer. Using this technique, 20 people with small tumours were picked up.[104] They all had their stomachs removed via a gastrectomy and they are doing well.[105] Those who do not have the mutation know their chances of contracting stomach cancer are drastically reduced. They no longer live in fear. A number of the family's lives have been extended because of the research. The early intervention means the chances of complete cure are very high. The research would not have happened if the research team had not taken the time to treat the family as equals in the search for what was causing the cancer that had taken too many of them early in their lives.

The key to the success of this research was that there was not a hint of deception or coercion, whereas in the Havasupai, Guaymi, Hagahai and Solomon Island projects there were significant degrees of deception. Onora O'Neill argues that 'it is of great significance to establish a fundamental human obligation to reject deception. This obligation provides the ethical basis for trustworthy action; and trustworthy action can provide important evidence for anyone who seeks to place trust'.[106] A commitment to rule out deception will have positive outcomes and, 'truthful communication, through care not to mislead, through avoidance of exaggeration, through simplicity and explicitness, through honesty in dealing with others, in a word through trustworthiness'.[107]

Healthcare researchers cannot exist without other people to do their research. Long, detailed ethics forms and scrutiny by ethics committees do not in themselves establish the trust that is necessary for research to be truly fruitful and ethical. Such trust can only be established by a frame of mind that treats those involved in the research as equals in every way. Treating these people as 'research subjects' who have given 'informed consent' may satisfy the massive bureaucracies that have been built up around ethics committees.[108] However, unless the researchers are prepared to equalise power with those who they carry out their research with, we will still be exposed to the risks of exploitation set out in this chapter. The commercial pressures for results, the academic pressures for publication and the status pressures to be the one to make the next breakthrough do not simply go away just because an ethics committee has signed off the research. In fact, once ethics committees have signed off, they normally have nothing more to do with the research. The ethics committee members can sleep easily in their beds at night knowing that all the little boxes have been ticked.

The reality is that unless the researchers work in a way that equalises power with those they work with, and build relationships of trust with them, ethics approval comes to nothing. It may well be that because of our obsession with ethics approval, researchers may spend more time filling out the ethics form and responding to enquiries from ethics committees than they do building the relationship of trust with those they are going to research with. My experience of being a research subject is that you are given an ethics form to sign and, after the research is complete, you never hear anything more. There is a strong sense of being used as a means to an end, rather than being part of something as an equal partner. If a relationship of trust is the essence of healthcare research, then it should be a requirement that the researchers provide evidence of equalising power with those they are carrying out research with.

Notes

1 Kantrowitz, A, 'America's First Human Heart Transplantation: The Concept, the Planning and the Furor', *ASAIO Journal* 44 1998, p 244; Henig, R, *Pandora's Baby: How the First Test Tube Babies Sparked the Reproductive Revolution*, New York: Houghton Mifflin Company, 2004, p 208.
2 Galloux, J *et al*, 'The Institutions of Bioethics', in Bauer, M and Gaskell, G (eds), *Biotechnology: The Making of a Global Controversy*, Cambridge: Cambridge University Press, 2002, pp 129–148, cites oncologist Van R. Potter as coining the term in 1971. They trace the history of bioethics from the 'discovery of genetic recombination techniques' in the 1970s. Galloux, J *et al* explain that bioethics developed within the scientific community and state at page 130 that it first evolved from the 'diverse and sometimes paradoxical anxieties within a scientific community trying to come to terms with the enormity of the power it was acquiring'.
3 Flynn, J, *How to Defend Humane Ideals*, London: University of Nebraska Press, 2000, p 25.
4 Ibid.
5 This has been most visible in the United States with the debate in legal circles between the Law and Economics movement and the Critical Legal Studies school. See generally, Minda, G, 'The Law and Economics and Critical Legal Studies Movements in American Law', in Mercuro, N (ed.), *Law And Economics*, Boston: Kluwer Academic Publishers, 1989, pp 87–122; Hutchinson, A and Monahan, P, 'Law, Politics, and the Critical Legal Scholars: The Unfolding Drama of American Legal Thought', *Stanford Law Review* 36, 1984, pp 199–245; Kennedy, D, 'Law-and-Economics from the Perspective of Critical Legal Studies', in Newman, P (ed.), *New Palgrave Dictionary of Economics and the Law*, New York: Macmillan, 1998, pp 465–474.
6 Op. cit., Flynn, J, p 27.
7 Leff, A, 'Unspeakable Ethics, Unnatural Law', *Duke Law Journal* 6, 1979, p 1229.
8 Op. cit., Flynn, p 68.
9 Jonsen, A, *The Birth of Bioethics*, New York: Oxford University Press, 1998; Wolpe, P, 'The Triumph of Autonomy in American Bioethics: A Sociological View', in DeVries, R and Subedi, J (eds), *Bioethics and Society: Constructing the Ethical Enterprise*, New Jersey: Prentice Hall, 1998.

10 McLean, S, *Modern Dilemmas: Choosing Children*, Edinburgh: Capercaillie Books, 2006; Freeman, M, 'Saviour Siblings', in McLean, S (ed.), *First Do No Harm*, London: Ashgate Publishing Ltd, 2006, pp 389–406.
11 O'Neill, O, *Autonomy and Trust in Bioethics*, Cambridge: Cambridge University Press, 2002, p 25.
12 Ibid.
13 Ibid.
14 Ibid.
15 *Havasupai Tribe v Arizona Board of Regents and Others* 22 Ariz. 214 204 P 3d 1063 (Ariz. 2008), p 1066.
16 Ibid.
17 Ibid.
18 Ibid.
19 Ibid.
20 Ibid, p 1067.
21 Ibid.
22 Ibid.
23 Ibid.
24 Ibid.
25 Ibid.
26 Ibid.
27 Ibid.
28 Ibid.
29 Ibid, pp 1067–1068.
30 Ibid, pp 1068–1070.
31 Pember, M, 'American Indians Grow Wary of Genetics Research', *Diverse: Issues In Higher Education*, 23 June 2010.
32 Ibid.
33 Harmon, A, 'Indian Tribe Wins Fight to Limit Research of Its DNA', *The New York Times*, 21 April 2010.
34 Ibid.
35 Harmon, A, 'Havasupai Case Highlights Risks in DNA Research', *The New York Times*, 21 April 2010.
36 Op. cit., Pember.
37 Ibid.
38 Ibid.
39 Ibid.
40 Posey, D and Dutfield, G, *Beyond Intellectual Property: Toward Traditional Resource Rights for Indigenous Peoples and Local Communities*, Ottawa: International Development Research Centre, 1996, p 26.
41 Ibid.
42 Ibid.
43 Op. cit., Posey and Dutfield, p 26.
44 Ibid.
45 Ibid.
46 Ibid.
47 Ibid.
48 Ibid.
49 Ibid.
50 Ibid.
51 Ibid.
52 Ibid.

53 Ibid, p 27.
54 Ibid.
55 Ibid.
56 ETC Group: Action Group on Erosion, Technology and Concentration, 'US Government Dumps the Hagahai Patent' (1996), ETC Group http://www. etcgroup.org/en/node/461.
57 Ibid.
58 Ibid.
59 Ibid.
60 Ibid.
61 Op. cit., Posey and Dutfield, p 27.
62 Ibid.
63 Ibid.
64 Ching, K, 'Indigenous Self-Determination in an Age of Genetic Patenting: Recognizing An Emerging Human Rights Norm', *Fordham Law Review* 66, 1997, pp 700–701.
65 Bhat, A, 'The National Institutes of Health and the Papua New Guinea Cell Line', *Genes, People and Property* 20, 1996 http://www.cultural survival.org.
66 Ibid.
67 Henaghan, M, *Genes, Society and the Future: Vol I*, Dunedin: Human Genome Research Project, 2007, p 17.
68 ' "Warrior gene" Blamed for Maori Violence', *The Age*, 8 August 2006 http://www.theage.com.au/news/National/Warrior-gene-blamed-for-Maori-viol ence/2006/08/08/1154802879716.html.
69 Ibid. See also, Lea, R and Chambers, G, 'Monoamine Oxidase, Addiction, and the "Warrior" Gene Hypothesis', *New Zealand Medical Journal* 120, 2007, pp 5–10, where Rod Lea retreats from the inferences drawn by the media.
70 Merriman, T and Cameron, V, 'Risk-Taking: Behind the Warrior Gene Story', *New Zealand Medical Journal* 120, 2007, p 59.
71 Ibid, pp 59–61. See also, Caspi, A *et al*, 'Role of Genotype in the Cycle of Violence in Maltreated Children', *Science* 297, 2002, pp 851–854; Kim-Cohen, J *et al*, 'MAOA, Maltreatment, and Gene-Environment Interaction Predicting Children's Mental Health: New Evidence and a Meta-Analysis', *Molecular Psychiatry* 11, 2006, pp 903–913; Spatz Widom, C and Brzustowicz, L, 'MAOA and the "Cycle of Violence": Childhood Abuse and Neglect, MAOA Genotype, and Risk for Violent and Antisocial Behavior', *Biological Psychiatry* 60, 2006, pp 684–689.
72 New Zealand Department of Corrections, *Annual Report 1 July 2004 – 30 June 2005*, Wellington: Department of Corrections, 2005, p 18. People who identify as Maori constitute only 14.5 per cent of the general population of New Zealand but those who identify as Maori make up 50 per cent of the prison population.
73 Tipene-Matua, B and Wakefield, B, 'Establishing a Maori Ethical Framework for Genetic Research with Maori', in Henaghan, M (ed.), *Genes, Society and the Future: Vol I*, op. cit., pp 379–422.
74 Op. cit., Henaghan, *Genes, Society and the Future: Volume I*, p 359. Citing Arbour, L and Cook, D, 'DNA on Loan; Issues to Consider When Carrying Out Genetic Research with Aboriginal Families and Communities', *Community Genetics* 9, 2006, pp 153–160.
75 Op. cit., Henaghan, *Genes, Society and the Future: Volume I*, p 17.
76 See, for example, Guilford, P *et al*, 'E-cadherin Germline Mutations in Familial Gastric Cancer', *Nature* 392, 1998, pp 402–405.

77 Tipene-Matua, B and the Rakaipaaka Health and Ancestry Study Management Team, 'Part Four: The Rakaipaaka Health and Ancestry Study: An Alternative Indigenous Response to Genetic Research', in Henaghan, M (ed.), *Genes, Society and the Future: Volume III*, Wellington: Brookers Ltd, 2009, p 202.
78 Ibid.
79 Ibid.
80 Ibid.
81 Ibid, p 203.
82 Ibid.
83 Ibid.
84 Ibid, pp 205–206.
85 Ibid, p 216.
86 Andrews, L and Paradise, J, 'Gene Patents: The Need for Bioethics Scrutiny and Legal Change', *Yale Journal of Health Policy, Law, and Ethics* 5, 2005, p 405.
87 Ibid. This patent was issued 21 October 1997.
88 Ibid, p 406.
89 Ibid.
90 Ibid, p 406. Citing Williams-Jones, B, 'History of a Gene Patent: Tracing the Development and Application of Commercial BRCA Testing', *Health Law Journal* 10, 2002, p 131.
91 Op. cit., Andrews and Paradise, p 406.
92 Ibid, p 407.
93 Ibid. Citing Knox, A, 'Companies Holding Patents to Disease-Related Genes Limiting Access', *Philadelphia Inquirer*, 13 February 2000.
94 Op. cit., Andrews and Paradise, pp 408–409.
95 Ibid, p 409. Citing Anand, G, 'Big Drug Makers Try to Postpone Custom Regimens', *The Wall Street Journal*, 18 June 2001.
96 See generally, McHugh, P, *The Maori Magna Carta: New Zealand Law and the Treaty of Waitangi*, Auckland: Oxford University Press, 1991; and Kawharu, I, *Waitangi: Maori and Pakeha Perspectives of the Treaty of Waitangi*, Auckland: Oxford University Press, 1989.
97 Henaghan, M and Mclean, S, 'Main Findings', in Henaghan (ed.), *Genes, Society and the Future: Volume 1*, op. cit., p 1.
98 Ibid.
99 Ibid.
100 Ibid.
101 Ibid.
102 Ibid.
103 Ibid.
104 Ibid.
105 Ibid.
106 Op. cit., O'Neill, p 97.
107 Ibid, p 98.
108 See generally, National Ethics Advisory Committee, 'Review of the Current Processes for Ethical Review of Health and Disability Research in New Zealand' (2004) National Ethics Advisory Committee http://www.neac.health.govt.nz/moh.nsf/indexcm/neac-resources-publications-reviewprocessesethicalresearch.

Chapter 7

Building trust into the healthcare system

So far, this book has analysed trust through the lens of individual healthcare professionals and researchers and their patients and research collaborators. Trust is also established by the perception of the healthcare system as a whole. That trust is built up by the thousands of interactions between healthcare professionals, patients and their families. That trust is based on how patients are treated, the results they receive, and the evenness of access and quality of care. Governments who want their healthcare system to be trusted across their communities need to listen to the voices of both patients and healthcare professionals.

International comparisons

The Commonwealth Fund in the United States has carried out invaluable research into the quality, access, efficiency, equality, mortality rates and healthy lives of citizens across a range of healthcare systems in Western countries.[1] The research is based on natural mortality data and the perceptions and experiences of patients and physicians. Medical records and administration data that could provide another view on the healthcare systems were not looked at. The perceptions of those surveyed are affected by their own expectations and experiences, which will vary from country to country.

What is most striking about the results is that whilst the United States spends the most *per capita* on healthcare ($US 7,290) it has ranked last or next to last overall in the 2004, 2006, 2007 and 2010 surveys.[2] The Netherlands, which was ranked first overall, spent $US 3,837 *per capita*; just over half of what the United States spends.[3] The United States fared best in 'provision and receipt of preventive and patient-centred care'.[4] Respondents in the United States were 'more likely than those in other countries to receive preventive care reminders and advice from their doctors on diet and exercise'.[5] This is an important element of establishing trust, which other countries can learn from. Atul Gawande, in his book *Better: A Surgeon's Notes on Performance*, points out that over five years, one woman in seven gets an annual mammogram, but over 10 years just one woman in 16 gets a mammogram.[6] Gawande says the underlying reasons are how 'time-consuming, uncomfortable and difficult it usually is to get a mammogram'.[7] He also says that over a billon dollars per year from government and private foundations is spent on research into new treatments for breast cancer, yet little is spent on innovations to improve the ease of mammography screening.[8] As Gawande points out, 'studies consistently show that more regular use of this one technology alone would reduce deaths from breast cancer by one-third'.[9]

According to the Commonwealth Fund study, the United Kingdom leads on the management of patients with chronic illnesses.[10] This is mainly because there has been a major push by the United Kingdom government to support and develop health information technology that enables healthcare professionals from the United Kingdom to print out a list of all their patients by diagnosis.[11]

The Netherlands ranked first in safe care, which is defined as 'avoiding injuries to the patients from the care that is intended to help them'.[12] Healthcare information technology is used 95 per cent of the time in the Netherlands to receive computerised alerts or prompts about potential problems with drug doses.[13] Incorrect medication doses and incorrect results from tests were rarest in the Netherlands.[14] The Netherlands ranks highest for having processes for identifying adverse events and taking actions to follow up.[15] The United States, Australia and Canada rank lowest for perception of medical error.[16] The threat of litigation in the United States does not appear to heighten potential perception of safety. It may be that a more litigious society creates higher expectations of error-free care. The Netherlands has put its faith in identifying adverse events and taking action to avert them. This is a better way of building trust into healthcare systems than the threat of legal action.

New Zealand leads the way in co-ordinating healthcare measures.[17] Primary care physicians receive information needed to manage a patient's care from the hospital within two weeks or less from when their patients are discharged.[18] Ninety-five per cent of patients in New Zealand have a regular doctor who co-ordinates care for them, whereas only 82 per cent of patients in the United States have a regular doctor.[19] A regular doctor builds up the trust of the patient by connecting them to other specialist help they may need.

New Zealand also ranked first in patient-centred care,[20] which is defined as 'care delivered with the patient's needs and preferences in mind'.[21] However, the research said that all countries 'could improve substantially in this area'.[22] The scores were low across the board in relation to whether doctors tell patients about treatment options and include patients in decisions about the best treatment for them.[23] New Zealand leads with 67 per cent of respondents saying their doctors did.[24] The United Kingdom was the lowest, at only 54 per cent, and the United States was next at 61 per cent.[25] Yet, 96 per cent of healthcare professionals from the United Kingdom said they routinely received data on patient satisfaction and experiences with care.[26] Only 23 per cent of healthcare professionals in the Netherlands received such feedback, yet they lead in overall satisfaction across all medicine,[27] which goes to show that regularly polling patients on satisfaction does not necessarily lead to patient-centred care. It is the actual care that counts, not a questionnaire check-up.

The Netherlands, the United Kingdom and Germany lead in good access to healthcare, which means patients can obtain affordable care and receive attention in a timely manner.[28] The United States fared much worse in access to healthcare because of cost. Fifty-four per cent of those surveyed in the United States said they had problems getting recommended tests, treatment and follow-up care, and visiting a doctor when they had a medical problem because of cost.[29] Fifty-eight per cent of physicians surveyed in the United States accepted that cost was a problem for many patients.[30] This research debunks the idea that universal or near universal healthcare provision was associated with long waiting times for care. Patients in Germany and the Netherlands were found to have the same rapid access to specialists as the highly insured patients from the United States.[31] The United States scored lowest in efficiency and maximising the expediency of care given the resources committed, with the United Kingdom scoring highest.[32] The United States duplicated tests more and patients visited hospital more, when a regular doctor could have treated them.[33] The Netherlands and the United Kingdom scored highest in overall 'equity',[34] which is defined as 'providing care that does not vary in quality because of personal characteristics such as gender, ethnicity, geographic location and economic status'.[35] This is a powerful measure of trust because it means treating people as equals. The United States scored lowest.[36] US citizens with below-average incomes were much more likely than their counterparts in other countries to report not visiting a physician when sick, not getting recommended tests or follow-up calls and not seeing a dentist because of cost.[37] Half of the lower-income adults surveyed in the US said they went without care because of cost.[38] At least 46 million citizens in the United States are uninsured.[39] The researchers found that 'even insured Americans and higher-income Americans were more likely than their counterparts in other countries to report problems such as not getting recommended tests, treatments, or prescription drugs'.[40]

The researchers conclude: 'Fragmented coverage and insurance instability undermines efforts in the US to improve care co-ordination, including the sharing of information among providers.'[41] The researchers believe that the enactment of the American Recovery and Reinvestment Act by the Obama administration, which will extend healthcare coverage to 32 million previously uninsured Americans, will lead to better outcomes and co-ordination.[42]

The overall results showed a strong relationship between performance in terms of equality and performance in other dimensions of quality – the lower the score for equality, the lower the performance in other measures. The research found that 'when a country fails to meet the needs of the most vulnerable, it also fails to meet the needs of the average citizen'.[43]

New Zealand healthcare inequality

The essence of equality is to treat everyone as an equal. As this book has shown, the essence of trust is to equalise power with others, particularly the most vulnerable. This idea not only builds trust at the individual level, but also builds trust in the healthcare system as a whole. Associate Professor Robin Gauld from the Department of Preventive and Social Medicine, and his medical trainee interns at the University of Otago, carried out research into the New Zealand healthcare system.[44] Using national and international data, the research found that 'New Zealand scored highest in efficiency (81%) and lowest in equality (58%)'.[45] New Zealand's low equality score was based on findings that there were 'vast differences in health measures depending on both ethnicity and socio-economic factors'.[46] An unequal healthcare system erodes trust on an individual level and in the system as a whole. It is promising that New Zealand's healthcare system is efficient, but it is of serious concern that New Zealand's healthcare system displays healthcare inequality based on ethnicity and socio-economic factors. This means New Zealand's healthcare system needs to equalise not just power between healthcare professionals and patients, but also between patients themselves.

Ivan Illich rightly points out that a 'world of optimal and widespread health is obviously a world of minimal and only occasional medical intervention'.[47] Illich goes on to say that, 'Healthy people are those who live in healthy homes on a healthy diet in an environment equally fit for birth, growth, work, healing and dying.'[48] New Zealand's healthcare system should cover all of these bases and enhance a person's all-round health. This requires trust and equality between all stakeholders in New Zealand's healthcare system.

A person's health should not be dependent upon their ethnicity or their socio-economic position. Unfortunately, however, many New Zealanders' health is affected by their socio-economic position. An extreme example of this is demonstrated by a Ministry of Social Development report into family violence-related homicides.[49] This report illustrates that children who live in homes that rank highly on the economic deprivation scale are at a significantly higher risk of being killed than children from families with greater economic means.[50] This is an extreme example, but it clearly shows that power needs to be equalised not just between healthcare professionals and patients, but also between patients themselves. New Zealand's healthcare system needs to be able to be used and trusted by all members of New Zealand society equally, regardless of socio-economic considerations.

To further enhance trust, New Zealand also needs to place a greater emphasis not just on providing quality healthcare treatment to patients once they are hurt or sick, but also on preventing patients from becoming sick in the first place. Ian Kennedy, in his book *The Unmasking of Medicine*, argues for greater emphasis on the prevention of illness and accidents and the general promotion of health.[51] This cannot be achieved by the healthcare system alone; rather, the government needs to provide significantly more support to prevent illness and accidents and to promote the overall health of all New Zealanders.

Alcohol consumption in New Zealand is a topical example of where the healthcare system needs more support from the government to enhance the health of all New Zealanders. Excessive alcohol consumption is fast being recognised as an unhealthy part of many New Zealanders' lives, which has a dramatic impact on the New Zealand healthcare system. Emergency departments throughout New Zealand are full of people, especially during the weekends, who have ended up hurting themselves, or getting hurt, because of alcohol.[52] A New Zealand Law Commission Report on the use of alcohol in New Zealand society illustrates the various serious healthcare problem and other harms caused by the excessive consumption of alcohol.[53] Based on these harms, the Law Commission made a series of recommendations to try to reduce and counter some of these harms.[54] To their credit, New Zealand doctors and nurses made strong submissions to the Law Commission.[55] Yet, because powerful commercial interests require excessive drinking to maximise their profits, the government has not been prepared to curb availability and advertising. Until the government is prepared to make more significant changes to New Zealand's alcohol laws, our healthcare system is left to pick up the pieces. This is not the best way to encourage trust and equality in New Zealand society.

Building trust

The core idea of this book is that, without trust, all the rights in the world do not matter. This is because rights and responsibilities go hand in hand. One person's right is dependent on another's responsibility. Patients have to trust healthcare professionals to fulfil their professional duties on a daily basis. Healthcare professionals have to trust their patients to give them accurate information about the patients' health. Trust is most likely to thrive where there is a 'welcoming of equalisation of power' between healthcare professionals and their patients. Care, empathy and respect for each other, as equals, are the central ingredients of trust in any healthcare system. These are internal attributes, which, once embedded, do not require external moderation. If care, empathy and respect are not internally embedded, then external moderation and auditing will make no difference. Compliance is not, and never could be, the same as choosing to treat others as one's equal.

The final words of this book are being written one month after the devastating earthquake in Christchurch, New Zealand on 22 February 2011, and during the aftermath of the shocking earthquake and tsunami in Japan on 11 March 2011. In both of these awful situations, emergency workers and healthcare professionals (as well as members of the public) put their own lives at risk to save others in need. The emergency workers and healthcare professionals did not endanger themselves to help others because they were required to do so by some kind of duty or external code of conduct, but simply because of the need to save people's lives.

A graphic example from the Christchurch earthquake was the way a team of emergency and healthcare professionals rescued an earthquake survivor by amputating both of his legs.[56] The patient was trapped in rubble after the quake and could not be extracted in any other way. In extreme circumstances, while aftershocks were still occurring, the healthcare professionals successfully anaesthetised the patient and amputated both the patient's legs using a builder's hacksaw and a Leatherman® pocketknife.[57] If the healthcare professionals had not intervened, the trapped man would have died. As one of the healthcare professionals involved said:

> The decision was made to remove the man's legs because he would have almost certainly died if we had delayed. He was continually bleeding, he would have bled to death. There was no way he was going to be extracted from the situation.[58]

These healthcare professionals (like many others during this tragedy) put their own lives at substantial risk to save a patient's life. The danger was very real; the healthcare professionals had to crawl into an unstable building during aftershocks and carry out a complex medical procedure in the dark without proper equipment. However, as one of the healthcare professionals said, 'Under the circumstances, that's just what you do: there was a life to be saved.'[59]

This kind of attitude and spirit does not need external audit. This kind of heroism inspires trust in healthcare professionals because it directly demonstrates empathy, compassion and respect for life. However, such an attitude should not be reserved solely for emergency situations. In order to be trusted, healthcare professionals should act with empathy, compassion and respect for life at all times. To further foster trust, they must also constantly equalise power between themselves and their patients. The everyday interactions between healthcare professionals and patients are of equal importance in fostering a culture of trust in our healthcare system. No amount of external auditing can foster empathy, compassion, respect for life and the equalisation of power. These qualities can only come from within healthcare professionals, and from within the healthcare profession itself.

Of course, trust is never a one-way street. The onus to foster trust lies not just with healthcare professionals, but also rests firmly on everyone involved. Patients, educators, governing bodies, policy makers, the government and healthcare professionals must all acknowledge their interdependence, and co-operate in growing and maintaining a culture of trust. It is hoped this book goes some way to placing trust at the forefront of healthcare training, practice and public health policy, so that all citizens can share the benefits of a more trustworthy healthcare system.

Notes

1 Davis, K, Schoen, C and Stremikis, K, *Mirror, Mirror on the Wall: How the Performance of the US Health Care System Compares Internationally*, New York: The Commonwealth Fund, 2010.
2 Ibid; Davis, K *et al, Mirror, Mirror on the Wall: Looking at the Quality of American Health Care Through the Patient's Lens*, New York: The Commonwealth Fund, 2004; Davis, K *et al, Mirror, Mirror on the Wall: An Update on the Quality of American Health Care Through the Patient's Lens*, New York: The Commonwealth Fund, 2006; and Davis, K *et al, Mirror, Mirror on the Wall: An International Update on the Comparative Performance of American Health Care*, New York: The Commonwealth Fund, 2007.
3 Op. cit., Davis, Schoen and Stremikis.
4 Ibid, p vi.
5 Ibid, p 5.
6 Gawande, A, *Better: A Surgeon's Notes on Performance*, London: Profile Books Ltd, 2007, p 233.
7 Ibid.
8 Ibid.
9 Ibid, p 234.
10 Op. cit., Davis, Schoen and Stremikis, p 5.
11 Ibid.
12 Ibid, pp 5–6.
13 Ibid, p 6.
14 Ibid.
15 Ibid.
16 Ibid.
17 Ibid, p 7.
18 Ibid, p 9.
19 Ibid, p 7.
20 Ibid, p 8.
21 Ibid, p 9.
22 Ibid.
23 Ibid, p 8.
24 Ibid.
25 Ibid.
26 Ibid, p 9.
27 Ibid, p 8.
28 Ibid, p 10.
29 Ibid, p 11.
30 Ibid.
31 Ibid, p 12.
32 Ibid, p 12.
33 Ibid.
34 Ibid, p 15.
35 Ibid, p 13.
36 Ibid, p 15.
37 Ibid, p 14.
38 Ibid.
39 Ibid, p 15.
40 Ibid, pp 16–17.
41 Ibid, p 17.
42 Ibid.

43 Ibid, p 18.
44 Goodwin, E, 'NZ Health System Gets Tick', *Otago Daily Times Online News*, 9 October 2010.
45 Ibid.
46 Ibid.
47 Illich, I, *Limits to Medicine: Medical Nemesis, the Expropriation of Health*, London: Marion Boyars, 1976, p 274.
48 Ibid.
49 Martin, J and Pritchard, R, *Learning from Tragedy: Homicide within Families in New Zealand 2002–2006*, Wellington: Ministry of Social Development, 2010.
50 Ibid, p 48.
51 Kennedy, I, *The Unmasking of Medicine*, London: George Allen and Unwin, 1981, pp 57–58.
52 Between 18 to 35 per cent of injury-based emergency department presentations are estimated to be alcohol related, rising to between 60 and 70 per cent during the weekends. Ministry of Health, 'Alcohol Quick Facts' (2010) National Drug Policy New Zealand http://www.ndp.govt.nz/moh.nsf/indexcm/ndp-publications-alcohol-factsheets.
53 The excessive consumption of alcohol by New Zealanders contributes to a range of serious harms including: an array of criminal offences, causative contribution to diseases (such as alcohol-related cancers, mental health disorders, foetal alcohol disorder and sexually transmitted infections), alcohol poisoning and accidental injury due to intoxication (sometimes causing death), harms to third parties (such as victims of crime, victims of domestic and family violence, children born into homes where adults drink to excess), harmful effects on educational outcomes, workplace productivity, friendships, social life, home life and financial positions, as well as public nuisance (such as litter, glass, noise damage and destruction of property and the costs associated with rectifying these nuisances). See generally, New Zealand Law Commission, *Alcohol in Our Lives: Curbing the Harm: A Report on the Review of the Regulatory Framework for the Sale and Supply of Liquor*, Wellington: New Zealand Law Commission, 2010.
54 The Law Commission made a series of recommendations including: introducing new legislation called the Alcohol Harm Reduction Act, increasing the price of alcohol through excise tax to reduce consumption, regulating promotions that encourage increased consumption, regulating alcohol advertising and sponsorship, increasing the purchase age of alcohol to 20 years old (it is currently 18 years old in New Zealand), strengthening the responsibility of parents supplying alcohol to minors, increasing personal responsibility for harmful behaviours induced by alcohol, cutting back the hours licensed premises are open, streamlining the enforcement of the new alcohol laws and placing the overall decision making with a new Alcohol Regulatory Authority, and improving and reorganising systems for the treatment of people with alcohol problems. See generally, op. cit., New Zealand Law Commission.
55 A group of New Zealand doctors and nurses banded together and recommended a set of policy directives as a guide to the Law Commission's review of the New Zealand liquor laws. The recommendations were to:

1   Raise alcohol prices;
2   Raise the purchase age;
3   Reduce alcohol accessibility;
4   Reduce marketing and advertising;
5   Increase drink-driving counter-measures;
PLUS: Increase treatment opportunities for heavy drinkers.

There are currently 324 healthcare professional signatories to this public statement. Alcohol Action New Zealand, 'An Historic Opportunity to Change New Zealand's Heavy Drinking Culture: A Public Statement by the Doctors and Nurses of New Zealand', http://alcoholaction.co.nz/resourcesandreferences.

Since the Law Commission Report, the government has introduced the Alcohol Reform Bill, which, as the explanatory note to the Bill states, implements the government's decisions on the reform of alcohol legislation. The policy objectives of the Bill are to:

- Reduce excessive drinking by young people and adults;
- Reduce the harm caused by alcohol use, including crime, disorder, public nuisance and negative public health outcomes;
- Support safe and responsible sale, supply and consumption of alcohol;
- Improve community input into local alcohol licensing decisions;
- Improve the operation of the alcohol licensing system.

Doug Sellman, Jennie Connor and Dr Geoffrey Robinson do not believe that the Alcohol Law Reform Bill has gone far enough in addressing the harms caused by alcohol in New Zealand society. As they state: 'There are four main things that we strongly want to see added to the Government's response to the Law Commission's review:

1 **End ultra-cheap alcohol,** beginning with a minimum price for a standard drink
2 **End highly normalised and accessible alcohol,** by restoring supermarkets to being alcohol-free
3 **End all alcohol advertising and sponsorship,** except objective printed product information
4 **End legal drink driving,** by reducing the adult blood alcohol level to 0.05 or below.'

See generally, Sellman, D, Connor, J and Robinson, G, *The New Alcohol Law Reform Bill: We Need More Than Just Tinkering With the Problem*, Christchurch: Alcohol Action NZ, 2011.

56 Johnston, M, 'Hacksaw Amputation "Just What You Do to Save a Life", Says Doctor', *The New Zealand Herald*, 26 February 2011.
57 Ibid.
58 Ibid.
59 Ibid.

Bibliography

Cases cited:

Alexandrou v Oxford [1990] EWCA Civ 19.
Capital & Counties Plc v Hampshire County Council [1997] EWCA Civ 3091, [1997] 3 WLR 331.
Donoghue v Stevenson [1931] UKHL 3, [1932] AC 562.
Gillick v West Norfolk and Wisbech Area Health Authority [1986] 1 AC 112 (HL).
Havasupai Tribe v Arizona Board of Regents and Others 22 Ariz. 214 204 P 3d 1063 (Ariz. 2008), p. 1066.
In Re F (Mental Patient: Sterilisation) [1990] 2 AC 1 (HL).
Jackovach v Yocom 237 NW 444 (Iowa 1931).
Kent v Griffiths & Ors [1999] Lloyd's Rep Med 424, p 456.
Kent v Griffiths & Ors [2000] EWCA Civ 25, [2000] 2 WLR 1158.
Lowns & Anor v Woods & Ors (1996) Australian Torts Reports 81–376 (NSWCA).
Malette v Shulman [1990] 72 OR (2d) 417.
Marshall v Curry [1933] 3 DLR 260, p 275.
OLL Ltd v Secretary of State for Transport [1997] 3 All ER 897.
R v Crawshaw HC Dunedin CRI-2005–012-001860, 6 March 2006, 'Notes of Evidence Taken Before the Honourable Justice Panckhurst and a Jury of Twelve'.
R v Dudley and Stephens [1884] 14 QBD 273.
R v Laufau [2001] NZLJ 82.
Rogers v Sells 61 P 2d 1018 (Okla 103).
Stovin v Wise [1996] UKHL 15, [1996] AC 923.
Woods & Ors v Lowns & Anor [1995] 36 NSWLR 344.

Legislation cited:

Accident Compensation Act 2001 (NZ).
Crimes Act 1961 (NZ).
Health and Disability Commissioner Act 1994 (NZ).
Health and Disability Commissioner (Code of Health and Disability Services Consumers' Rights) Regulations 1996 (NZ).
Health Practitioners Competence Assurance Act 2003 (NZ).
Medical Practitioners Act 1995 (NZ).

Medical Practitioners Act 1938 (NSW).
Medical Practitioners Act 1992 (NSW).
Mental Health (Compulsory Assessment and Treatment) Act 1992 (NZ).
National Health Service (General Medical Services Contracts) Regulations 2004 (UK).
New Zealand Bill of Rights Act 1990 (NZ).
Nurses Amendment Act 1990 (NZ).

Works cited:

Abel, R, 'Restoring Trust', in *Lawyers in the Dock*, New York: Oxford University Press, 2008.
Ahern, M and Hendryx, M, 'Social Capital and Trust in Providers', *Social Sciences and Medicine* 57, 2003.
Alcohol Action New Zealand, 'An Historic Opportunity to Change New Zealand's Heavy Drinking Culture: A Public Statement by the Doctors and Nurses of New Zealand, Alcohol Action New Zealand http://alcoholaction.co.nz/resourcesandreferences.
American Medical Association, 'Opinion 8.12 – Patient Information', *Code of Medical Ethics*, March 1981.
Anand, G, 'Big Drug Makers Try to Postpone Custom Regimens', *The Wall Street Journal*, 18 June 2001.
Andrews, L and Paradise, J, 'Gene Patents: The Need for Bioethics Scrutiny and Legal Change', *Yale Journal of Health Policy, Law, and Ethics* 5, 2005.
An Inquest into the Death of Isabell Grace Riddell, Coroners Court Hamilton 970506, 24 April 1997.
Ansley, B, 'Mind That Child', *New Zealand Listener* 3080, 1999.
Arbour, L and Cook, D, 'DNA on Loan; Issues to Consider When Carrying Out Genetic Research with Aboriginal Families and Communities', *Community Genetics* 9, 2006.
Atiyah, P, *The Damages Lottery*, Oxford: Hart Publishing, 1997.
Baier, A, *Moral Prejudices: Essays on Ethics*, Cambridge, MA: Harvard University Press, 1994.
Bailey, T, 'On Trust and Philosophy', BBC Reith Lectures: The Philosophy of Trust, 2002 http://www.open2.net/trust/on_trust/on_trust1.htm.
Bain, J and Foster, M, 'Should the Doctor Come?', *Proceedings of the Medico-Legal Society* 6, 1976–80.
Barefoot, J *et al*, 'Trust, Health and Longevity', *Journal of Behavioural Medicine* 21, 1998.
Barnes, M, 'Blunt Instruments: Medicine, Law and the Death of Nancy Lim', http:www.nancylim.org.
Berlinger, N, *After Harm: Medical Error and the Ethics of Forgiveness*, Baltimore: Johns Hopkins University Press, 2005.
Bhat, A, 'The National Institutes of Health and the Papua New Guinea Cell Line', *Genes, People and Property* 20, 1996 http://www.cultural survival.org.
Bismark, M and Paterson, R, 'No-Fault Compensation in New Zealand: Harmonizing Injury Compensation, Provider Accountability, and Patient Safety', *Health Affairs* 25, 2006.

Blommestein, H, 'How to Restore Trust in Financial Markets?', in Dembinski, P *et al* (eds), *Enron and World Finance: A Case Study in Ethics*, New York: Palgrave MacMillan, 2006.

Brooks, B and Rizzo, A, 'Catholic Church: Shuffling Priests Around the Globe', *Buenos Aires Herald*, 18 April 2010 http://www.buenosairesherald.com/BreakingNews/View/30996.

Brown, C, 'Deterrence in Tort and No Fault: The New Zealand Experience', *California Law Review* 73, 1985.

Brunton, W, 'The Origins of Deinstitutionalisation in New Zealand', *Health and History* 5, 2003.

Bryer, L, *A History of the 'Unfortunate Experiment' at National Women's Hospital*, Auckland: Auckland University Press, 2009.

'Bushfire Doctor Shows Value of Locum Work', *Rural Healthcare Australia*, 2009.

Cabot, R, 'The Use of Truth and Falsehood in Medicine: An Experimental Study', *American Medicine* 5, 1903.

'Cancer-Stricken Boy Tried to Jump From Car: Mother', *New Zealand Herald*, 22 August 2000.

Cartwright, S, *The Report of the Cervical Cancer Inquiry 1988,* Auckland: Government Printing Office, 1988.

Caspi, A *et al*, 'Role of Genotype in the Cycle of Violence in Maltreated Children', *Science* 297, 2002.

Ching, K, 'Indigenous Self-Determination in an Age of Genetic Patenting: Recognizing An Emerging Human Rights Norm', *Fordham Law Review* 66, 1997.

Clark, H, 'PM Welcomes Governor-General-Designate', www.beehive.govt.nz, 24 August 2000.

Collins, D and Brown, C, 'The Impact of the Cartwright Report upon the Regulation, Discipline and Accountability of Medical Practitioners in New Zealand', *Journal of Law and Medicine* 16, 2009.

Collins, F, *The Language of God: A Scientist Presents Evidence for Belief*, New York: Free Press, 2006.

Coney, S and Bunkle, P, 'An "Unfortunate Experiment" at National Women's', *Metro*, June 1987.

Cornford, F, *The Republic of Plato*, London: Oxford University Press, 1970.

Couric, K, 'Haiti's 21st Century Makeshift Hospital', *CBS News*, 23 April 2010.

Crawford, B *et al*, *Review of the Quality, Safety and Management of Maternity Services in the Wellington Area*, Ministry of Health, 2008.

Cronin, A, *Dr Finlay's Casebook*, London: BBC, 1962.

Croskerry, P, 'Achieving Quality in Clinical Decision Making: Cognitive Strategies and Detection of Bias', *Academic Emergency Medicine* 9, 2002.

———, 'The Importance of Cognitive Errors in Diagnosis and Strategies to Minimize Them', *Academic Medicine* 78, 2003.

———, 'The Theory and Practice of Clinical Decision-Making', *Canadian Journal of Anaesthesia* 52, 2005.

Cunningham, W, 'The Medical Complaints and Disciplinary Process in New Zealand: Doctors' Suggestions for Change', *New Zealand Medical Journal* 117, 2004.

Cunningham, W, Crump, R and Tomlin, A, 'The Characteristics of Doctors Receiving Medical Complaints: A Cross-Sectional Survey of Doctors in New Zealand', *New Zealand Medical Journal* 116, 2003.

Cunningham, W and Dovey, S, 'The Effect on Medical Practice of Disciplinary Complaints: Potentially Negative for Patient Care', *New Zealand Medical Journal* 113, 2000.

Cunningham, W and Wilson, H, 'Shame, Guilt and the Medical Practitioner', *New Zealand Medical Journal* 116, 2003.

Davis, P *et al*, 'Compensation for Medical Injury in New Zealand: Does "No-Fault" Increase the Level of Claims Making and Reduce Social and Clinical Selectivity?', *Journal of Health Politics, Policy and Law* 27, 2002.

Davis, K *et al*, *Mirror, Mirror on the Wall: Looking at the Quality of American Health Care Through the Patient's Lens*, New York: The Commonwealth Fund, 2004.

——, *Mirror, Mirror on the Wall: An Update on the Quality of American Health Care Through the Patient's Lens*, New York: The Commonwealth Fund, 2006.

——, *Mirror, Mirror on the Wall: An International Update on the Comparative Performance of American Health Care*, New York: The Commonwealth Fund, 2007.

——, *Mirror, Mirror on the Wall: How the Performance of the US Health Care System Compares Internationally*, New York: The Commonwealth Fund, 2010.

Day, K, 'Medical Negligence – The Duty to Attend Emergencies and the Standard of Care: *Lowns & Anor v Woods & Ors*', *Sydney Law Review* 18, 1996.

de Montesquieu, Baron C, *The Spirit of the Laws*, in Cohler, A, Miller, B and Stone, H (trans.), Cambridge: Cambridge University Press, 1989.

Department of Statistics, *New Zealand Official Yearbook 1982*, Wellington: Department of Statistics, 1982.

Dewees, D, Duff, D and Trebilcock, M, *Exploring the Domain of Accident Law: Taking the Facts Seriously*, New York: Oxford University Press, 1996.

Director of Proceedings v Thomas Paul O'Flynn, Medical Practitioners Disciplinary Tribunal, 291/03/110D 15 July 2004 http://www.mpdt.org.nz/decisionsorders/precis/03110d.asp.

'DNR', Season 1, Episode 9, *House*, Los Angeles: Fox Broadcasting Company, 2004.

Duffy, A, Barrett, D and Duggan, A, *Report of the Ministerial Inquiry into the Under-Reporting of Cervical Smear Abnormalities in the Gisborne Region*, Wellington: Committee of Inquiry Report, 2001.

Dyer, C, 'GP Faces 15 Charges of Murder', *British Medical Journal* 319, 1999.

Ely, J *et al*, 'Malpractice Claims Against Family Physicians: Are the Best Doctors Sued More?', *Journal of Family Practice* 48, 1999.

ETC Group: Action Group on Erosion, Technology and Concentration, 'US Government Dumps the Hagahai Patent', ETC Group, 1996 http://www.etcgroup.org/en/node/461.

'Family Weep at Cancer Boy Verdict', *New Zealand Herald*, 24 August 2000.

Fanaeian, N and Merwin, E, 'Malpractice: Provider Risk or Consumer Protection?', *American Journal of Medicine Quality* 16, 2001.

Fehr, E and Gächter, S, 'Cooperation and Punishment in Public Goods Experiments', *American Economic Review* 90, 2000.

Flynn, J, *How to Defend Humane Ideals*, London: University of Nebraska Press, 2000.

Frazer, W, 'Milton Friedman and Thatcher's Monetarist Experience', *Journal of Economic Issues* 16, 1982.

Freeman, M, 'Saviour Siblings', in McLean, S (ed.), *First Do No Harm*, London: Ashgate Publishing Ltd, 2006.

——, *The Rights and Wrongs of Children*, London: F. Pinter, 1983.

Freud, S, *New Introductory Lectures in Psycho-Analysis*, London: The Hogarth Press, 1977.

Friedman, M, *Capitalism and Freedom*, Chicago: University of Chicago Press, 1962.

Galloux, J et al, 'The Institutions of Bioethics', in Bauer, M and Gaskell, G (eds), *Biotechnology: The Making of a Global Controversy,* Cambridge: Cambridge University Press, 2002.

Gambetta, D (ed.), *Trust: Making and Breaking Cooperative Relations*, New York: Blackwell Publishers, 1990.

Gandhi, T et al, 'Missed and Delayed Diagnoses in the Ambulatory Setting: A Study of Closed Malpractice Claims', *Annals of General Medicine* 145, 2006.

Gawande, A, *Better: A Surgeon's Notes on Performance*, London: Profile Books Ltd, 2007.

Gilbert, J, *Breach of Faith, Breach of Trust,* New York: iUniverse, 2010.

Gillett, G, 'Doctor Does Not Always Know Best', *Otago Daily Times*, 16 September 2010.

Goeltz, R, 'For My Brother', *National Patient Safety Foundation Newsletter* 3, 2000.

Goodwin, E, 'Surgeon Criticises ACC Savings Drive', *Otago Daily Times*, 3 April 2010.

——, 'NZ Health System Gets Tick', *Otago Daily Times Online News*, 9 October 2010.

Gray, J, *False Dawn: The Delusions of Global Capitalism,* London: Granta Publications, 1998.

Groopman, J, *How Doctors Think*, Melbourne: Scribe Publications, 2007.

Grubb, A, 'Medical Negligence: Liability of Ambulance Service', *Medical Law Review* 8, 2000.

Guilford, P et al, 'E-cadherin Germline Mutations in Familial Gastric Cancer', *Nature* 392, 1998.

Haines, L, 'Another Unfortunate Experiment', *New Zealand Listener* 217, 2009.

Hansard (8 December 1987) 485 NZPD 1619.

Hardin, R, *Trust and Trustworthiness*, New York: Russell Sage Foundation, 2002.

Harmon, A, 'Havasupai Case Highlights Risks in DNA Research', *The New York Times*, 21 April 2010.

——, 'Indian Tribe Wins Fight to Limit Research of Its DNA', *The New York Times*, 21 April 2010.

Haynes, A et al, 'A Surgical Safety Checklist to Reduce Morbidity and Mortality in a Global Population', *The New England Journal of Medicine* 360, 2009.

Hayward, R et al, 'Sins of Omission: Getting Too Little Medical Care May Be the Greatest Threat to Patient Safety', *Journal of General Internal Medicine* 20, 2005.

Health and Disability Commissioner, *Southland District Health Board Mental Health Services: February–March 2001*, Invercargill: Health and Disability Commissioner, 2002.

——, *Midwife, Ms B; Midwife, Ms C*, Case 04HDC05503, 28 November 2006.

——, *Midwife, Mrs B: A Rural Maternity Hospital*, Opinion 07HDC16053, 10 June 2008.

——, *Annual Report of the Health and Disability Commissioner for the Year Ended 30 June 2009*, Auckland: Health and Disability Commissioner, 2009.

Health Systems Research Inc, *Bioterrorism and Other Public Health Emergencies – Altered Standards of Care in Mass Casualty Events*, Rockville: Agency for Healthcare Research and Quality, 2005.

Heller, J, 'Syphilis Victims in the US Study Went Untreated for 40 Years', *The New York Times*, 26 July 1972.

Henaghan, M (ed.), *Genes, Society and the Future: Volume I*, Dunedin: Human Genome Research Project, 2007.

——, *Genes, Society and the Future: Volume III*, Dunedin: Human Genome Research Project, 2009.

Henaghan, M and Mclean, S, 'Main Findings', in Henaghan, M (ed.), *Genes, Society and the Future: Volume 1*, Dunedin: Human Genome Research Project, 2007.

Henaghan, M and Righarts, S, 'Public Perceptions of the New Zealand Court System: An Empirical Approach to Law Reform', *Otago Law Review* 12, 2010.

Henig, R, *Pandora's Baby: How the First Test Tube Babies Sparked the Reproductive Revolution*, New York: Houghton Mifflin Company, 2004.

Henzell, D, 'The Good Doctor with a Damaged Reputation', *Sunday Star Times*, 25 July 2004.

Hippocrates, 'Epidemics', in Jones, W (trans.), *Hippocrates Volume I*, Cambridge: Harvard University Press, 1948.

——, 'Decorum', in Jones, W (trans.), *Hippocrates Volume II*, Cambridge: Harvard University Press, 1952.

——, 'Aphorisms', in Jones, W (trans.), *Hippocrates Volume IV*, Cambridge: Harvard University Press, 1953.

Holt, R, 'Making Difficult Ethical Decisions in Patient Care During Natural Disasters and Other Mass Casualty Events', *Otolaryngology – Head and Neck Surgery*, 139, 2008.

Holton, R, 'Deciding to Trust, Coming to Believe', *Australasian Journal of Philosophy* 72, 1994.

'Hospital Arrives in Aceh as Logjam Delays Aid', *The Sydney Morning Herald*, 8 January 2005.

Hume, D, *A Treatise of Human Nature*, Selby-Bigge, L and Nidditch, P (eds), Oxford: Clarendon Press, 1978.

Hutchinson, A and Monahan, P, 'Law, Politics, and the Critical Legal Scholars: The Unfolding Drama of American Legal Thought', *Stanford Law Review* 36, 1984.

Illich, I, *Limits to Medicine: Medical Nemesis, the Expropriation of Health*, London: Marion Boyars, 1976.

Institute of Medicine, *To Err is Human: Building a Safer Health System*, Washington: National Academy Press, 2000.

Ipp, D, *Review of the Law of Negligence*, Canberra: Commonwealth of Australia, 2002.

Johnston, M, 'Cancer Boy Dies After Lack of Care', *New Zealand Herald*, 25 August 2000.

——, 'Hacksaw Amputation "Just What You Do to Save a Life", Says Doctor', *New Zealand Herald*, 26 February 2011.

Jones, J, *Bad Blood: The Tuskegee Experiment*, New York: The Free Press, 1981.

Jonsen, A, *The Birth of Bioethics*, New York: Oxford University Press, 1998.

Kahneman, D, Slovic, P and Tversky, A (eds), *Judgment Under Uncertainty: Heuristics and Biases*, Cambridge: Cambridge University Press, 1982.

Kahneman, D and Tversky, A, 'Subjective Probability: A Judgment of Representativeness', *Cognitive Psychology* 3, 1972.

Kantrowitz, A, 'America's First Human Heart Transplantation: The Concept, the Planning and the Furor', *ASAIO Journal* 44 1998.

Kassirer, J and Kopelman, R, 'Cognitive Errors in Diagnosis: Instantiation, Classification, and Consequences', *The American Journal of Medicine* 86, 1989.

Katz, J, *The Silent World of Doctor and Patient*, New York: Free Press, 1984.

Kawharu, I, *Waitangi: Maori and Pakeha Perspectives of the Treaty of Waitangi*, Auckland: Oxford University Press, 1989.

Kennedy, D, 'Law-and-Economics from the Perspective of Critical Legal Studies', in Newman, P (ed.), *New Palgrave Dictionary of Economics and the Law*, New York: Macmillan, 1998.

Kennedy, I, *The Unmasking of Medicine*, London: George Allen and Unwin, 1981.

Kim-Cohen, J *et al*, 'MAOA, Maltreatment, and Gene-Environment Interaction Predicting Children's Mental Health: New Evidence and a Meta-Analysis', *Molecular Psychiatry* 11, 2006.

Kirch, W and Schafii, C, 'Misdiagnosis at a University Hospital in 4 Medical Eras: Report on 400 Cases', *Medicine* 75, 1996.

Kmietowicz, Z, 'Complaints Against UK Doctors Rise 50 Per Cent', *British Medical Journal* 322, 2001.

Knox, A, 'Companies Holding Patents to Disease-Related Genes Limiting Access', *Philadelphia Inquirer*, 13 February 2000.

Kuriyama, S, 'Interpreting the History of Bloodletting', *Journal of the History of Medicine and Allied Sciences* 50, 1995.

Laing, R, *The Politics of the Family, and Other Essays*, London: Routledge, 1998.

Larkin, N, 'Parents' Agony Over Son They Loved to Death', *New Zealand Herald*, 25 August 2000.

Laugesen, R, 'Flying Blind', *New Zealand Listener* 3643, 2010.

——, 'Just Checking', *New Zealand Listener* 3643, 2010.

Lea, R and Chambers, G, 'Monoamine Oxidase, Addiction, and the "Warrior" Gene Hypothesis', *New Zealand Medical Journal* 120, 2007.

Leff, A, 'Unspeakable Ethics, Unnatural Law', *Duke Law Journal* 6, 1979.

Luhmann, N, *Trust and Power*, Chichester: John Wiley & Sons, 1979.

Machiavelli, N, *The Prince*, London: Penguin Books, 2003.

Maier, M, 'Afghan Security Forces Gain 52 New Doctors and Nurses', *NATO Training Mission–Afghanistan*, 18 April 2010.

Martin, J and Pritchard, R, *Learning from Tragedy: Homicide within Families in New Zealand 2002–2006*, Wellington: Ministry of Social Development, 2010.

McHugh, P, *The Maori Magna Carta: New Zealand Law and the Treaty of Waitangi*, Auckland: Oxford University Press, 1991.

McInnes, M, 'The Question of a Duty to Rescue in Canadian Tort Law: An Answer from France', *Dalhousie Law Journal* 13, 1990.

McLean, S, *Modern Dilemmas: Choosing Children*, Edinburgh: Capercaillie Books, 2006.

McEvoy, V, 'The Incredibles', *Harvard Medical Alumni Bulletin* 79, 2006.

McGoogan, E, *Review of Progress to Implement the Recommendations of the Gisborne Cervical Screening Inquiry Report*, Wellington: Office of the Auditor General, 2002.

Meadow, W, Bell, A and Lantos, J, 'Physicians' Experience With Allegations of Medical Malpractice in the Neonatal Intensive Care Unit', *Paediatrics* 99, 1997.

Medical Practitioners Disciplinary Tribunal, *In the Matter of Jacobus Petrus de la Porte*, Decision 70/98/38C, 24 March 1999.

Merriman, T and Cameron, V, 'Risk-Taking: Behind the Warrior Gene Story', *New Zealand Medical Journal* 120, 2007.

Minda, G, 'The Law and Economics and Critical Legal Studies Movements in American Law', in Mercuro, N (ed.), *Law And Economics*, Boston: Kluwer Academic Publishers, 1989.

Ministry of Health, 'History of Health and Disability Ethics in New Zealand', Health and Disability Ethics Committees, 2007 www.ethicscommittees.health.govt.nz.

——, 'Alcohol Quick Facts', National Drug Policy New Zealand, 2010 http://www.ndp.govt.nz/moh.nsf/indexcm/ndp-publications-alcohol-factsheets.

——, *Statement of Intent 2010–13*, Wellington: Ministry of Health, 2010.

National Ethics Advisory Committee, 'Review of the Current Processes for Ethical Review of Health and Disability Research in New Zealand', National Ethics Advisory Committee, 2004 http://www.neac.health.govt.nz/moh.nsf/indexcm/neac-resources-publications-reviewprocessesethicalresearch.

New Zealand Department of Corrections, *Annual Report 1 July 2004 – 30 June 2005*, Wellington: Department of Corrections, 2005.

New Zealand Law Commission, *Alcohol in Our Lives: Curbing the Harm: A Report on the Review of the Regulatory Framework for the Sale and Supply of Liquor*, Wellington: New Zealand Law Commission, 2010.

O'Neill, O, *Autonomy and Trust in Bioethics*, Cambridge: Cambridge University Press, 2002.

——, *A Question of Trust: The BBC Reith Lectures 2002*, Cambridge: Cambridge University Press, 2002.

Oppenheim, R, 'Resource Allocation and Clinical Negligence Claims', *Clinical Risk* 10, 2004.

Palmer, E, 'Resource Allocation, Welfare Rights – Mapping the Boundaries of Judicial Control in Public Administrative Law', *Oxford Journal of Legal Studies* 20, 2000.

Paterson, R, 'The Patients' Complaints System in New Zealand', *Health Affairs* 21, 2002.

Paul, C *et al*, 'A Survey of Attitudes to Parent–Doctor Conflicts Over Treatment for Children', *The New Zealand Medical Journal* 114, 2001.

Pearson, C, *Report of the Royal Commission on Civil Liability and Compensation for Personal Injury*, London: Her Majesty's Stationery Office, 1978.

Pember, M, 'American Indians Grow Wary of Genetics Research', *Diverse: Issues In Higher Education*, 23 June 2010.

Permatasari, S and Sukarsono, A, 'Indonesian Doctors Struggle as Quake Death Toll Rises', *Bloomberg Press*, 2 October 2009.

Plato, 'Lysis', in Hamilton, E and Cairns, H (eds), *The Collected Dialogues of Plato*, Princeton: Princeton University Press, 1961.

Pollitt, C, 'The Struggle for Quality: The Case of the National Health Service', *Policy and Politics* 21, 1993.

Pope, A, *An Essay on Criticism*, 1709.

Pope Benedict XVI. *Pastoral Letter of the Holy Father Pope Benedict XVI to the Catholics of Ireland*, 2010 http://www.vatican.va/holy_father/benedict_xvi/letters/2010/documents/hf_ben-xvi_let_20100319_church-ireland_en.html.

'Pope Failed to Act on Sex Abuse', *BBC News*, 25 March 2010 http://news.bbc.co.uk/2/hi/8587082.stm.

Posey, D and Dutfield, G, *Beyond Intellectual Property: Toward Traditional Resource Rights for Indigenous Peoples and Local Communities*, Ottawa: International Development Research Centre, 1996.

Power, M, *The Audit Explosion*, London: Demos, 1996.

Redelmeier, D, 'The Cognitive Psychology of Missed Diagnoses', *Annals of Internal Medicine* 142, 2005.

Reiter, S and Williams, P, 'The Philosophy and Rhetoric of Auditor Independence Concepts', *Business Ethics Quarterly* 14, 2004.

Reverby, S, *Examining Tuskegee: The Infamous Syphilis Study and its Legacy*, Chapel Hill: The University of North Carolina Press, 2009.

Roberts, P, *Snakes and Ladders: The Pursuit of a Safety Culture in New Zealand Public Hospitals*, Wellington: Health Services Research Centre, 2003.

Robertson, B, *Adams on Criminal Law Student Edition*, Wellington: Brookers, 2009.

Robertson, G, *The Case of the Pope: Vatican Accountability for Human Rights Abuse*, New York: Penguin, 2010.

Rogers, D, 'On Trust: A Basic Building Block For Healing Doctor–Patient Interactions', *Journal of the Royal Society of Medicine* 87, 1994.

Royal College of Physicians, *Trust in Doctors 2009: Annual Survey of Public Trust in Professions*, London: Ipsos MORI, 2009.

Sachs, J, *Common Wealth: Economics for a Crowded Planet*, London: Penguin Books, 2009.

'SAF Team in Afghanistan', *The Straits Times*, 2 April 2010.

'Samoa Hospital Sees Post-Tsunami Sanitation and Food-Related Illness', *Radio New Zealand*, 7 October 2009.

Sauviat, C, 'The Demise of Andersen: A Consequence of Corporate Governance Failure in the Context of Major Changes in the Accounting Profession and the Audit Market', in Dembinski, P *et al* (eds), *Enron and World Finance: A Case Study in Ethics*, New York: Palgrave MacMillan, 2006.

Schwartz, A and Elstein, A, 'Clinical Reasoning in Medicine', in Higgs, J *et al* (eds), *Clinical Reasoning in the Health Professions*, 3rd edn, Sydney: Elsevier, 2008.

Seligman, A, *The Problem of Trust*, Princeton: Princeton University Press, 1997.

Sellman, D, Connor, J and Robinson, G, *The New Alcohol Law Reform Bill: We Need More Than Just Tinkering With the Problem*, Christchurch: Alcohol Action NZ, 2011.

Skegg, P, 'Consent to Treatment: Introduction', in Skegg, P and Paterson, R (eds), *Medical Law in New Zealand*, Wellington: Brookers Ltd, 2006.

Smillie, J, 'The Future of Negligence', *Tort Law Journal* 15, 2007.

Smith, J, *The Shipman Inquiry Volume 1: Death Disguised*, Manchester: The Shipman Inquiry, 2002.

Sox, H, 'The Ethical Foundations of Professionalism: A Sociologic History', *Chest: Official Publication of the American College of Chest Physicians* 131, 2007.

Spatz Widom, C and Brzustowicz, L, 'MAOA and the "Cycle of Violence": Childhood Abuse and Neglect, MAOA Genotype, and Risk for Violent and Antisocial Behavior', *Biological Psychiatry* 60, 2006.

'Specialist Blasts System Failures in Cancer Boy Case', *New Zealand Herald*, 23 August 2000.

Statistics New Zealand, 'National Population Estimates: December 2005 Quarter, 2006   http://www.stats.govt.nz/browse_for_stats/population/estimates_and_projections/national-population-estimates-info-releases/previous-releases.aspx.

Sternberg, S, 'Revelation a Reminder of Era of Abuse', *Otago Daily Times World Focus*, 4–10 October 2010.

Summerton, N, 'Trends in Negative Defensive Medicine Within General Practice', *British Journal of General Practice* 50, 2000.

Surowicki, J, *The Wisdom of Crowds: Why the Many Are Smarter Than the Few*, New York: Anchor Books, 2005.

Sztompka, P, 'Trust in Democracy and Autocracy', in *Trust: A Sociological Theory*, Cambridge: Cambridge University Press, 1999.

Tallis, R, *Hippocratic Oaths: Medicine and its Discontents*, London: Atlantic Books, 2005.

Tarn, D *et al*, 'Physician Communication When Prescribing New Medications', *Archives of Internal Medicine* 166, 2006.

The Health and Social Care Information Centre, 'Data on Written Complaints in the NHS 2008–2009', The Information Centre for Health and Social Care, 2009 http://www.ic.nhs.uk/statistics-and-data-collections/audits-and-performance/complaints/data-on-written-complaints-in-the-nhs-2008–09.

The Leading Edge, '2008 New Zealand's Most Trusted Professions', *Reader's Digest Magazine*, 2008.

——. 'Australia's Most Trusted Professions 2008', *Reader's Digest Magazine*, 2008.

The Royal Australian and New Zealand College of Obstetricians and Gynaecologists, *Maternity Services Review Submission*, 31 October 2008.

Tipene-Matua, B and the Rakaipaaka Health and Ancestry Study Management Team, 'Part Four: The Rakaipaaka Health and Ancestry Study: An Alternative Indigenous Response to Genetic Research', in Henaghan, M (ed.), *Genes, Society and the Future: Volume III*, Wellington: Brookers Ltd, 2009.

Tipene-Matua, B and Wakefield, B, 'Establishing a Maori Ethical Framework for Genetic Research with Maori', in Henaghan, M (ed.), *Genes, Society and the Future: Volume I*, Dunedin: Human Genome Research Project, 2007.

Travis, A, 'Enron *et al* and Implications for the Auditing Profession', in Dembinski, P *et al* (eds), *Enron and World Finance: A Case Study in Ethics*, New York: Palgrave MacMillan, 2006.

'Trust in Catholic Church Plummets Amid Abuse Scandal', *The Local: Germany's News in English*, 24 March 2010 http://www.thelocal.de/society/20100324–26081.html.

Tversky, A and Kahneman, D, 'Availability: A Heuristic for Judging Frequency and Probability', *Cognitive Psychology* 4, 1973.

United States Senate Hearing, 'Patient Safety: Instilling Hospitals with a Culture of Continuous Improvement', 11 June 2003.

Vallance, G, 'Ethical Issues in Obtaining Informed Consent and the Right to Refuse Treatment in the Emergency Context', *Otago Bioethics Review*, 1996.

Wall, T, 'Liam Case Worried Mangere Boy Carers', *New Zealand Herald*, 15 October 1999.

——, 'Parents Put Boy's Cancer into Hands of God', *New Zealand Herald*, 12 October 1999.

' "Warrior gene" Blamed for Maori Violence', *The Age*, 8 August 2006 http://www.theage.com.au/news/National/Warrior-gene-blamed-for-Maori-violence/2006/08/08/1154802879716.html.

Weinrib, E, 'The Case for a Duty of Rescue', *The Yale Law Journal* 90, 1980.

Weycker, D and Jensen, G, 'Medical Malpractice Among Physicians: Who Will be Sued and Who Will Pay?', *Health Care Management Science* 3, 2000.

Wilkinson, R and Pickett, K, *The Spirit Level: Why More Equal Societies Almost Always Do Better*, London: Allen Lane, 2009.

Williams, K, 'Litigation Against English NHS Ambulance Services and the Rule in *Kent v Griffiths*', *Medical Law Review* 15, 2007.

Williams-Jones, B, 'History of a Gene Patent: Tracing the Development and Application of Commercial BRCA Testing', *Health Law Journal* 10, 2002.

Wolpe, P, 'The Triumph of Autonomy in American Bioethics: A Sociological View', in DeVries, R and Subedi, J (eds), *Bioethics and Society: Constructing the Ethical Enterprise*, New Jersey: Prentice Hall, 1998.

Woodhouse, O, *Compensation for Personal Injury in New Zealand: Report of the Royal Commission of Inquiry*, Wellington: Government Printer, 1967.

World Health Organization. 'Surgical Safety Checklist', Safe Surgery Saves Lives, 2009 www.who.int/patientsafety/safesurgery/en/.

World Medical Association General Assembly. *The World Medical Association Statement on Medical Ethics in the Event of Disasters*, Stockholm: World Medical Association General Assembly, 1994.

Youngson, R, Wimbrow, T and Stacey, T, 'A Crisis in Maternity Services: The Courage to be Wrong', *Quality and Safety in Health Care* 12, 2003.

Zimbardo, P, *The Lucifer Effect: Understanding How Good People Turn Evil*, New York: Random House, 2007.

Index

'A Modern Version of the Hippocratic
    Oath' 69
Accident Compensation Act 45, 59, 74
Accident Compensation Corporation
    (ACC) 59, 61
*After Harm: Medical Error and the Ethics
    of Forgiveness* 64
all-knowing philosophy 63, 64
American Recovery and Reinvestment
    Act 126
apology 72–3
audit 6–7, 9
autonomy 108
Autonomy and Trust in Bioethics 101

Baier, A. 16, 23–4
Bailey, T. 26
Better: A Surgeon's Notes on Performance
    79, 124
'Big Day Out' 93, 94
*Bioterrorism and Other Public Health
    Emergencies – Altered Standards of Care
    in Mass Casualty Event* 38

Cabot, R. 67
cardiopulmonary resuscitation 23
Cartwright, S. 8
Cartwright Report 2, 12
checks and balances theory 56
chrome-endoscopy technique 119
Code of Consumers' Rights 1, 31, 33
Code of Medical Ethics of American
    Medical Association 65–6
common law 31, 35, 40
complaints: healthcare professional's
    feeling of shame and guilt 62–4;
    patient's feelings of not being
    listened to and ignored 64–6;

patterns of 61; perceptions of 61–6;
    trends 57–61
complaints processes 56–81; apology,
    72–3; complaints trends 57–61;
    disclosure 71–2; forgiveness 74–5;
    healthcare professionals do not know
    it all 66–71; patterns of complaints
    61; perception of complaints 61–6;
    rebuilding trust 66; reduction of
    opportunities to betray trust and
    incentives for creation of trusted
    environment 79–81; repentance
    73–4; simplifying and quickening
    the process 75–9; theory of distrust
    56–7
consultants 19
'consumer' 31
Crawshaw, J. 90–1
Croskerry, P. 70–1

Declaration of Helsinki (1964) 21
defensive medicine 61
'diabetes-centered project' 109
disclosure 71–2

emergency situation 30–50; basing
    situation on trust 43–4; classification
    30–2; failure to act in emergency
    circumstances 38–42; justification for
    acting without consent 32–8; legal
    duty 44–50
equalisation of power 24

Flynn, J. 108
forgiveness, 74–5

Gambetta, D. 25
Gauld, R. 127